EARTHBORN WISDOM

UNDERSTANDING SYMBOLOGY OF THE EVERYDAY WORLD

by
Susan Wells

Illustrated by
Steve Goins

DREAMTIME PUBLISHING

Library of Congress Cataloging-in-Publication Data
Wells, Susan
Illustrated by: Steve Goins
Earthborn Wisdom:
Understanding Symbology of the Everyday World
        A compilation of stories and conversations with animals. Practical wisdom is conveyed to aid the reader to understand common problems and issues from a new perspective.

ISBN No.-0-9741726-0-X   Price: $12.95
1. Self-help 2. Spirituality 3. Native American studies 4. Myths and Legends 5. Storytelling

Library of Congress Catalog Card Number
99-076965
Manufactured in the United States of America

Dedicated to
"Willie" Wells,
my "Little Brother,"
my Teacher, my friend,
who gave me the gift of myself.

CONTENTS
PART 1

PART 2 EARTH CHILD

PART I

EARTHBORN

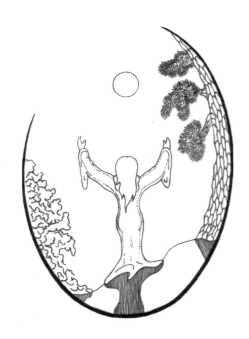

INITIATION

As we go through life, we are taught that symbols have meaning. A popular version of this is the phrase about something being a "sign." Native American people understand this concept. They also have a sense of humor about the way the principles of symbolic meaning are so casually used.

When driving with a Native American shaman, we passed a billboard with a hawk perched on top. He turned to me and said, "You know what that is?"

I said, "What?"

"It's a sign!" He answered, and burst out laughing.

During our lives, we assign meaning to many things, using them to help guide our growth and learning. This man, who could laugh at the casual understanding of this aspect of life, lives his life by signs and symbols that speak to him, and in one brief statement expressed how he feels such things are being trivialized by the "pop" culture.

There are currently many books and people available to tell us what different objects are supposed to mean. There can be some value in using these prepared patterns. However, when we assign meaning to anything using the dictates of another's experience we deny our own being and add to our own insecurities. We are accepting the premise that someone else knows better than we do about our own existence and reality. In popular terms, we are giving our power away and weakening our sense of self.

Following any teaching presented as fact empowers the teacher, not ourselves.

And, there is a subtle difference between someone "teaching" us something and the experience of learning. We all have experiences in our lives that enable us to build our own symbology and create a framework that has true meaning in our lives.

Finding our own meaning derived from personal experiences empowers ourselves, and when we use our own experiences to learn and grow, the process as well as the results become our own.

I was extremely stressed about money. Driving down a country road I was lost in severe worry about how I could possibly get myself out of my financial hole. Suddenly, an entire flock of about 30 redbirds flew directly in front of my windshield, startling me. Along with them came a wash of comfort and confidence that the money thing would work itself out. From this incident, redbirds became a symbol to me, and I've found that whenever I begin being concerned about money, one, or several redbirds will fly in front of me (even in cities) and it always feels like a tap on my shoulder, reminding me I need not worry, it will all work out.

This is from my OWN experience! No one told me this is what redbirds mean. Redbirds do not symbolize this to anyone else I know. But this is what they mean to me!

This book is not meant to tell you what different animals mean or what they might have to say to you. It is an attempt to show you a way of developing your own personal symbology by giving you the context in which I developed some of my own, and how that symbology applied to my life. It is meant to be a tool for learning how to use your own experience to create your own meaningful symbols in your life and empower yourself.

This is what "Medicine" is all about.

Medicine is a catalyst that helps things happen. Something that brings about change and healing. We have explanations of how and why medicines work that satisfy our intellect. However, the effects remain in the world of magic. Sometimes they work and sometimes they don't. Pure physical manipulation of illnesses or injuries does not automatically produce the results desired. Healing seems to require a kind of inner cooperation on a spiritual level in order for it to be effective.

The "medicine" that brings about these inner changes producing real differences in our lives exists on an even more mystical plane. The very intangibility of this kind of medicine has caused it to be rejected in many circles. Some of its forms have been all but lost.

In Native American circles the definition of medicine includes the idea of learning and growth along with physical healing. Medicine involves putting the spirit right with life and having the inner changes manifest outwardly in healing. In fact, the inner rightness has more relevance than what may be seen on the surface. Working with this inner rightness is a constant part of life and includes sharing with and learning from many natural elements—one of which is animals. Animals are brothers who, by sharing their wisdom and guidance as well as their special skills in survival, can help with the problems of living and being, and can become powerful symbols in our lives. It is recognized that each animal has unique perspectives in its lifestyle that can help us understand ourselves better. This wisdom is an essential part of Native American teaching, where life lessons often come from animals.

Even people not of this belief system can understand how a special connection can be established with an animal. Usually it is experienced with a pet of some kind... a particular animal that was able to give us something we found nowhere else. To accept the concept of having a definite communication with that animal is not only comfortable, it is almost an unspoken fact that each individual knows in his heart. There are many accepted explanations of this phenomenon, such as reading the body language of the animal or the sounds it makes having specific meanings, but there is always a deeper feeling that there is more than that going on. There is a basic acceptance that the animal somehow understands us and responds to our needs. It is an integral part of why the animal is important to us and they come to have deep symbolic meaning in our lives. Expanding this understanding to the point of realizing that all animals have characteristic "somethings" to offer is another matter entirely.

Most of our culture has turned away from any conscious connection with nature so that the idea of communicating with animals has largely been forgotten or ignored. It is not that animals speak such a difficult language. On the contrary, their language consists of images and feelings for the most part. It may be that man's avoidance of his own true feelings has contributed to shutting him off from such communication. At any rate, the images and feelings from animals can become a clearer communication if the door is allowed to open and we begin to listen with our hearts rather than our ears or culturally rigid minds. If we relax with the idea, and accept that these *may* actually be communications from the animals, the images and feelings begin to translate naturally into words we can work with.

I encourage you to take the time to quiet yourself, allowing your heart to hear what they have to offer you. This is a book of my own experience and is by no means the totality of what they have to give. What you hear may be different lessons entirely. But perhaps this book can assist you in knowing how to listen, as well as expand your awareness of the types of teaching they offer. Crack the door of your mind—experiment—you too can learn the language if you allow yourself to be open to it.

And, remember that animals are only one potential area for symbols and messages. There is a world of plants, and stones, and many other things that can become meaningful symbols or signs in your life and used for your personal growth, development and healing. If we allow ourselves to believe in miracles of all sizes, anything can happen.

BUZZARD

Once the buzzard was an eagle and he had feathers on his head. Like all other eagles he hunted and killed for food. But buzzard flew clumsily and often missed his kill. It was after such a miss that he sat thinking about why the other eagles were so good at killing and he was not. As he thought, he began to realize the difference. The other eagles were warrior spirits who found honor in the natural process of killing, and pride in doing it well and cleanly. And he saw that their way was right for them. However, as he reached inside himself for understanding he realized that he did not like to kill. The more he searched within himself the less he wanted to kill, for when he killed he could feel the fear and pain of the animal and he did not like being a part of this kind of energy in the world. Yet, if he did not kill, he would die. He did not know what to do, so he decided to go on a vision quest.

He flew to a perch on a high mountain, spread

his wings, and called out to the Great Spirit:

"Great Spirit, I am weary of the killing. I am not comfortable causing fear and pain. Surely, there must be another way that I might be of service. Let me remove fear and pain, not cause it. The earth needs more gentleness and understanding, not more pain, fear and death. I ask that you show me a different way, for I cannot go on as I have any longer. If my existence means more killing, pain and fear, then let my existence end, for I will not kill again."

And there he sat, with his wings outstretched in prayer, waiting for an answer or death.

The Great Spirit heard his prayer and appeared before him as a purple/white flame saying, *"You have spoken from your heart. To have what you ask you must put your head into the flame."*

The Buzzard hesitated, not knowing whether this meant change or death, but he knew he must do this and so he thrust his head into the fire. The flame leaped higher and he felt the burning as he experienced the pain of all he had known leaving him. Still, he held his head in the flame and allowed the process to occur. Gradually the flame subsided and Buzzard knew what the Great Spirit wanted him to do. His nature was that of a flesh eater, but he would no longer kill. Instead he would eat only that which was already dead. The flesh he consumed would be changed within his body to energy and strength as always. However, now he would also consume the animal's pain and fears which he would change into love, understanding and wisdom within him.

Then Buzzard came down from the mountain. He was found by the other birds eating a long-dead rabbit. The other birds began to laugh and tease him, *"What are you doing? Where are the feathers on your head? Have you lost your mind along with your feathers?"*

Buzzard said nothing, but stopped eating, for this was a sacred ceremony, and he flew away. Then the other birds stopped laughing and their mouths opened in awe.

For as Buzzard soared gracefully in his flight they sensed that he had been touched by the Great Spirit and his life had been given purpose and meaning. They no longer laughed at him or his ways after that. He was given quiet respect and honor.

This is Buzzard Medicine.

Whenever any of us are in the process of trying to change ugly things within us into something beautiful, call on the Buzzard. He knows how to change ugliness of any kind into beauty and he will help you.

THE VISIT

I learned about the changing qualities of Buzzard from a medicine sister who works with it a great deal. She explained that the Buzzard worked by transmuting that which is repulsive into beautiful flight.

After learning this I decided to ask the Buzzard for help when I was working with some aspects of my environment that needed transmuting. In a prayerful state I "called" and almost immediately the Buzzard essence and energy was very strong, imaging itself clearly in my mind. I was so surprised by his appearance that I broke from my intent and focus saying, "You feel like Buzzard, but you have feathers on your head. Buzzards don't have feathers, they are bald."

The Buzzard answered, *"Never mind now, we have work to do. I will tell you the story another time."*

I returned to my intent and focus and we completed the work. I completely forgot about what he had said until I was driving between Tulsa and Wichita and Buzzard "appeared" again. He filled the car and rode with me telling his story. When he'd finished and he was sure that the details were clear in my mind the way he intended them, he continued to ride with me and I asked him if there was more he had to say.

"Man can use our help, but he doesn't understand our medicine. Help us to reach those of your kind so they will know how we can help them."

I found the idea exciting and began thinking about how to put his words on paper so that they could communicate the ideas and feelings he'd given me. And still he rode with me.

"Is there more?" I asked.

Quietly, he added, *"There are others. You've had*

others tell you things."

I thought of my experiences with the Spider and the Dolphin.

"They would like help in reaching your kind as well—and there will be more.

"It is important for man to understand our ways and realize how we can help. Translate for us so we can share with them in their own language, until they again learn ours."

Now, when animals "speak" to me, I try to listen even more carefully than before so I can translate as clearly as possible—placing their message and, more importantly, their intent on paper. The following chapters recount some of these experiences that have occurred since then.

SPIDER

I felt called to the woods. As I walked through familiar terrain I noticed there were an unusual number of spider webs in the area. After running into four or five of them I stopped and asked if the spider was trying to get my attention.

I sensed a leap of joy as the air around me filled with spider essence. So I sat on a log and waited to find out why the spider had called me. Spiders generally give me a prickly, uneasy feeling. This was no different because it was the essence of spider that surrounded me and seemed to take form before me, saying,

"You have much to learn, my dear. And we will begin with lessons of the web.

"There is beauty in what we do." The image of many spider webs glistening with dew in the morning sun entered my mind and I remembered how often I'd remarked on how beautiful they were.

"First, my dear, in spinning the web we spin dreams, hopes and goals into threads we create out of our own beings. The web we spin is the very substance of life. We are aware that our webs are often damaged or torn apart—sometimes," she smiled, *"by clumsy people. It is simply the way of things. We don't worry about it we just spin another.*

For it is the process of creating, the effort of reaching for perfection, where life is found. It doesn't matter whether the thing we create is perfect or permanent. That is what maintenance is for, repairing and improving the patterns as we go, and removing things that don't belong, keeping the pattern in order.

"Second, there is the lesson of trust. We spin our web and wait. We have done our part and know that the universe will provide. Sometimes what is provided is bountiful, and sometimes it is sparse. But always it is enough. We know to store some of the bounty to avoid waste. However, this is not done out of fear, only out of respect, for we know there will always be enough.

"Third is the lesson of acceptance. We accept what the universe sends to our web. Some of what is sent are tastier than others. And some, like wasps, are equal to us and have stings of their own capable of killing us. We deal with all of these situations the same: We use our skill and agility to accomplish what the universe gave us to do. We know there is purpose in all things no matter how much effort it takes to meet the challenges given us. We simply apply the amount of effort the task requires.

"You too spin webs, my dear. You put yourself in what you do and think and dream. Be careful of the patterns you spin. Some patterns will not hold up under the natural stresses of things.

"Be careful where you anchor your main lines. Make sure the bases you use are solid.

"Take your time in making your webs so that the patterns are even and balanced.

"Do not worry if your webs become broken or torn. Do not worry even if they are destroyed. Simply begin spinning again, either to repair an old pattern or to begin a new one. It is the process that matters.

"The universe takes care of you too, just continue to do your part.

"Accept the challenges your web brings you, and do what you need to do to meet the challenges. Your skill

and agility will be adequate to handle what the universe gives you to do.

"We will always help you with your webs if asked. Yes, even if you remove us from your house... as long as there is acknowledgment and respect in the process.

"Speak to my little ones and ask them to leave. If they do not, or cannot, they will understand. Your house is part of your web and we understand the importance of keeping it in order.

"Now, I think you've had enough lessons for today, though there are many more to give you. You see, we spiders helped to spin the universe and we understand many things.

"However, I see your mind is full for now. Consider what I've told you and perhaps we'll talk again."

The prickly sense faded, the air seemed different, and the spider essence was gone.

I had a new respect for spider energy even though I was still uncomfortable with it. However, I also felt that perhaps my discomfort had more to do with their efficiency and meticulous attention to detail than from anything negative about them.

ANT

In the past several weeks ant has presented itself to speak, but the timing was wrong or other priorities kept putting it off. The ant did not seem in a hurry, he just kept tapping me on the shoulder every so often, reminding me that he also had things to say.

Then one night after I had gone to bed, ant came forth and insisted that now was the time, so I arose to focus on his message.

"We are known to be workers. This is only a small part of what we have to offer you. Perseverance is common in nature.

"Patience is another matter. Most things are not completed as rapidly as man wants them to be. Yet when he talks of patience he often means letting other forces decide when and how something is to be done, giving away the active part of accomplishing, and allowing himself to become merely a building block in the structure of things.

"Patience does not mean losing the dynamic essence of being. It is not passive. It is a matter of actively pursuing while accepting that there is a quality of timing involved. Patience does not mean giving up your power. It means applying your power in the most productive way. It is recognizing that foundations and preparation are important if anything is to

have a sound structure. This applies to the internal building of self as well as any tangible structure.

"Remaining aware is important too. You need to know when the timing is appropriate to seize the moment.

"Stamina and endurance is a factor in all of this as well. Continue actively pursuing your goals in the face of seeming setbacks and delays and the power of patience will begin to have more meaning.

"Man has forgotten his own real power. He thinks it is so remarkable that we can move and carry objects larger than ourselves even though man has the same kind of capacity. It is not a question of physical strength, it is a question of clarity. Man's true essence can accomplish feats way beyond himself, no less dramatic than ours. Man needs only to forget the idea of being limited and simply do it. Man tells himself things are hard and he believes it. If he merely recognized that something takes effort instead of believing it is hard, he would accomplish more.

"Man has also forgotten the value of help. Two can do more than one and one. Man loses this concept in wanting his own way. He seems to fear that he will be lost if he allows himself to be a part. If he were more sure of his own being this would not be a problem.

"We live as a community. We work together. There is nothing lost of ourselves in the process, and we function much better as a whole. Man too is a social being, but until he begins to understand his true nature he will continue to have problems with his own kind."

Ant grew quiet. I felt he had more to say, but he had backed off for now, and again I was left with much to think about.

SQUIRREL

OK! OK! OK!

I have been going along trying to get my work done, but squirrel keeps poking his nose in everything I do, chattering at me. If I don't stop to listen I won't get a thing done!

The squirrel twitched his tail and said, *"You seem annoyed with me.*

"It is this energy in you that has drawn me to you to explain a few things.

"Squirrels are never really very still— we play as hard as we work. But the intensity of our irritation is what I've come to discuss with you

"Squirrels can sit and scream half the day away in annoyance at a cat, or a bird, or anything that disrupts what we want to do. We use all that time not playing, not storing nuts for winter, not tending to business—just screaming.

"You watch the squirrels and laugh at such a spectacle, how they waste their time and use up so much energy accomplishing nothing.

"Why do you take yourself so seriously?"

Good question. Why do I?

SNAKE

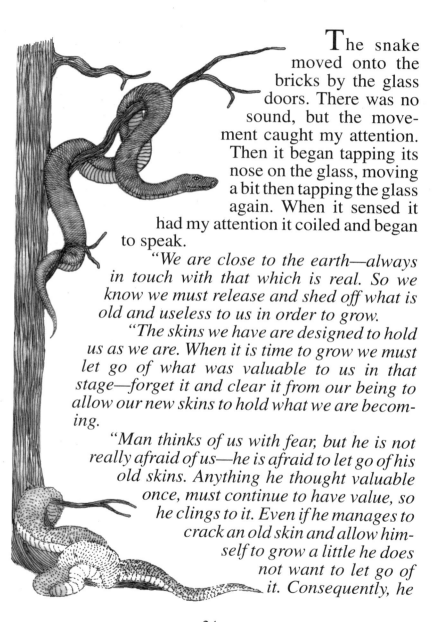

The snake moved onto the bricks by the glass doors. There was no sound, but the movement caught my attention. Then it began tapping its nose on the glass, moving a bit then tapping the glass again. When it sensed it had my attention it coiled and began to speak.

"We are close to the earth—always in touch with that which is real. So we know we must release and shed off what is old and useless to us in order to grow.

"The skins we have are designed to hold us as we are. When it is time to grow we must let go of what was valuable to us in that stage—forget it and clear it from our being to allow our new skins to hold what we are becoming.

"Man thinks of us with fear, but he is not really afraid of us—he is afraid to let go of his old skins. Anything he thought valuable once, must continue to have value, so he clings to it. Even if he manages to crack an old skin and allow himself to grow a little he does not want to let go of it. Consequently, he

goes around carrying all this dead stuff—afraid that if he puts any of it down he will lose something of value. So his old skins accumulate and stifle him.

"Of course, we have to laugh at the image he creates with all these old skins hanging loosely and peeling away around him like petals of a dead flower. Our laughter doesn't increase man's affection for us in the least, but it is a sympathetic laugh, for we also understand the awkwardness of a skin that is difficult to remove.

"Call on us—we would be glad to help you work on shedding your old skins more effectively."

Somehow it never occurred to me that snakes might have a sense of humor! But as I thought of the images that had been presented, I could feel those old skins still attached, flopping in the breeze as I moved. I could also feel how the gentle humor of the image was already helping to loosen them.

DOLPHIN

As I sat in medicine prayer I was surrounded by dolphins, swimming around me as though the ether were water.

"Breathe like a dolphin," they said.

"What does that mean?" I asked. "How does that apply?"

The first response was many images flowing through my mind and wordless concepts taking shape.

Then they said, *"Water is the element we live in even though our natural element is air. We rise to the surface to fill our beings with the air we need to survive and then dive into the water where we live, finding food to sustain our bodies. You are like us, your spirit must be fed, and where it finds food is outside the element of emotion. Yet you live and feed your bodies in a world of emotion.*

"Reach into the world of spirit, fill your lungs and then hold your spirit breath as you dive into the world in which you live. You are part of that watery emotional world. You function in it, and you feed your bodies there. However, if we try to breathe the water we will die, and if you try to take in the world of emotion as you would spirit, it will destroy you.

"Accept where you live, but understand your nature—feed that which needs to be fed

26

in the world where it finds appropriate food."

They took me deep into the ocean and I asked, "We are so deep. What if we need air and the surface is too far away?"

They laughed and said, *" Then you need the kiss of the Dolphin." And they showed me two dolphins linked mouth to mouth.*

"How does that help?" I asked.

A dolphin came to me and placed his mouth on mine and we shared air. I felt refreshed, almost as though I had gone to the surface. I floated in wonder at what I'd experienced as they explained.

"Find one of your own kind and share your spirit until you can find the surface again..

"Remember to breathe like a dolphin and you will keep yourself in balance. You will also have a clearer perspective on what is happening around you."

And with that the dolphins faded and I returned to where I began—with a new perspective on who I was.

MOUSE

There is a mouse in the house. I have tried to deal with it reasonably, but I can no longer tolerate the food loss and contamination and I have reached my limits cleaning up leftover mouse on my counters and in my cupboards. Still, I don't like the idea of traps. Mouse spirit, how can I handle this appropriately?

"The mouse in your house has touched your world with his whiskers. Outside he is food for many and risks are high. He is now living in the illusion that he has found heaven. A safe harbor with no threats and all kinds of food—enough to last him for a lifetime. Is man so different? He constantly seeks a state of being that has no risk. Man works his whole lifetime trying to establish an environment where he can live in luxury with no threat, no fear—and it is just as much of an illusion. Life is constant risk on all dimensions. Your mouse should not take so much effort to understand.

"Reach out to him

with your mind and tell him that there is plenty of food outside. Tell him that the risks he encounters there are ones that are natural for him and are in harmony with his being. Inform him that he does not belong where he is and that you are setting a trap that will mean certain death for him, a death that will not fulfill his purpose. Tell him that if he does not leave and go back to his natural way of being that his life will be wasted."

I did what the mouse spirit had told me to do. I set the trap and I talked to the mouse. I was not sure that this would work, but I felt a little clearer in my conscience.

By the end of the week the trap was still not sprung, but there were no signs of mouse anywhere. My mind again turned to the mouse essence—grateful for the guidance I'd received, and feeling a certain wonder at how simple things could be when approached through an attitude of harmony. I also began looking at some of the unnecessary risks I had in my own life coming from reaching for illusions of safety.

MORE SPIDER

I find spider wandering into what I do. As I live and experience she whispers things into my ear:

"In working on your web, my dear, you only see a small part of the whole pattern. You focus on that single part but you must also sense a larger pattern at the same time. You should know that this small part of yours needs to fit appropriately so that the whole pattern will function well. Remember this while working on your own part. Focus on having your part of the pattern strong, clear and clean, for as you make your connections you link with other webs and the strength of your pattern may affect many others, whether you know it or not."

"When reaching to extend your web, try as many times as it takes. Remember the larger pattern—sense what is needed—if it is right, continue trying until you succeed. When the pattern is right it is worth every effort it requires to complete it. Try. Try just once more—and once more again—until the connection is made.

"An ill-constructed pattern can still work. However, as you link your web with others it will cause undue stress on the overall pattern. So, before expanding your web, make sure the pattern you've constructed is strong. The further you extend your web, the more important it becomes to have a balanced pattern. If the web is not strong and balanced the more complex stresses can break connections, both within your web and those you are attempting to make.

"Sometimes connec-

tions will break when other unbalanced patterns connect with you. However, if you are within your strength and balance your pattern will not be affected severely."

So many details... but that is just the surface. I can feel beneath the details a firm message to maintain my endurance. That I need not worry about getting the product perfect, just keep trying. Don't give up just because it becomes difficult, or because it is not progressing the way I thought it would... or thought it ought to. Just keep working to make it better.

TURTLE

There have been many turtles on the road, and I met one in the woods today while I was gathering herbs. It seems there are things he wants to say.

"My kind lives with the illusion that our shell will protect us. We carry it awkwardly, hiding within at any sign of danger.

"It only works with threats of no consequence. You've seen how a wolf can crack our shell with ease. A determined foe with any intelligence can end all thoughts of safety.

"We have other defenses. Our shell is really the last resort and very shortsighted.

"Man creates shells for himself that are just as awkward and just as useless in the face of any real threat.

"Safety is not a goal that is worth the effort. There is no such thing. Real threats usually give very little warning. Relying on a shell that gives the illusion of safety may be the quickest and surest path to your destruction.

"We are not as bright, or quick, or powerful as many of the other animals, yet my kind has survived a long time by moving slowly, and being aware of our environment, responding to whatever is happening now. We have learned to understand the powers we have.

"For example: we have learned how to be invisible.

"There are many ways to deal with life. Survival requires more than a mechanical use of any approach. It requires an active aware-

ness. You cannot create a protective shield to life, either materially or mentally. You can only respond to what is next."

But, without shields I will be open and vulnerable!

Of course__we all are anyway! Hiding only keeps us from developing the skills needed to cope with the pressures of change and perceived threats. It weakens us so that we do not have the ability to act appropriately when necessary.

RABBIT

Someone very dear to me was passing a kidney stone. We did not know that was what it was as I sat with him in the emergency room of the hospital. I only knew there was something dramatically wrong and my fear was tangibly devouring my sense of things in spite of my efforts to cope with what was happening. Suddenly, the essence of Rabbit filled my mind.

"Attitude is ALL!

"My kind understand this. Have you not seen us trembling in fear calling our own death? Yet we have the strength in our legs to kick a coyote senseless. We have claws that can rip an enemy to pieces. And we have speed and agility to flee from almost any pursuer.

"It is seldom the coyote that kills us. It is our own fear. We need only to choose life over death!"

I could feel a calmness, an objectivity in the center of my fear, and my efforts to cope shifted ground.

BAT

For days a sense of "something" had been traveling with me. My feeling was that another animal was wishing to speak, yet when I focused on it there was only a sense of passive entity— a large blob of gray with enormous power and strength. My mind connected strength with size and came up with bear, but that didn't feel right. Then it reached hard, "Elephant?" I sensed nothing but a vague sense of a smile.

No, this was not the way. To force the issue puts my ego and distortion into the matter rather than having it be their message. Pushiness isn't polite, it shows no respect. That was something they had already shown me. So I backed off. They would speak in their own good time and it had nothing to do with my impatience or time schedule.

Slowly, in its own time, the blob of gray did take shape. I looked at the face—it looked like a mouse only much bigger and my mind flashed on the giant mouse in Sylvester cartoons.

Then a light exploded in my head, "BAT!" And I could see the detail of its face and wings. I knew little of bats and wondered what an animal so strange to me would have to say.

A wave of gentleness and wisdom flowed over me.

"I am considered sightless. How do I fly?"

I felt as though a door were opening in my head.

"I live in what you would call darkness without the mechanical aid of eyes. Yet I fly and hunt more quickly and surely than sighted beings. My sight is inward. I see myself clearly, and in doing so I do not need eyes to function.

"Because I am in tune with my surroundings I sense where to be and what to do and trust that implicitly.

"When I return home I go inward to maintain my clarity, for if I lose touch with who I am, I am lost.

"As I go inward I connect myself with spirit, and attach myself to part of the earth for balance. I hang upside down to make sure I keep connected with the earth, so I do not go too far into spirit and forget where I am.

"The universe has intricate patterns of energy that shift and flow in currents. When you become clear with who you are you too can move with them. Your sense of where to be and what to do becomes second nature. There is no question. You are there and doing before you have a chance to think about it. If I tried to think where I needed to fly I would run into a tree. If I had any doubt, if I began to wonder how I fly without eyes, I would easily convince myself that I couldn't do it.

"Man has forgotten how to move with the currents. He began to wonder how he did it, and looked for explanations of how it worked. He began telling himself that if he did not know how, he must not be able to. When man began to doubt, he ran into trees. His answer was to ask for more proof so he could figure out how to make it work. Now the proofs have limited him to only a narrow part of the working universe.

"Most people are frightened of us. They give many reasons why, but the real reason is that we remind them of what they've given up. Their spirit remembers and longs for what we have, while their minds tell them they cannot do it.

"Yet, if they reach inward and touch their own spirit, honestly looking at what they have embraced for so long, they can remember.

"Man does not need the mechanics of thought to function. Man only needs to sense the currents of energy that are part of nature to know where to be and what to do.

"Man's ways are uncertain, even with all his proofs. He is fearful and moves constantly trying to cover all possibilities with his mind. His way of being based on proofs has brought him no peace, and still he clings to it.

"We can help you remember. Our way is simple and clean. We move in harmony with what is. To relearn the harmony of nature that is outside of the limited way man has insisted on, it will mean change.

"It will mean a deeper honesty than man is used to. It will mean thinking and feeling in a completely different way. It will mean seeing the truth of himself. Seeing the truths that he has put so much effort into hiding from himself.

"It is man's nature to fly without fear as we do. However, to do so he must remember who he is. He must remember that knowing is not a thing of the mind, it is a thing of the heart.

"When he truly remembers he can once again dance on the wind."

The bat was suddenly gone, leaving me very much aware of how I still try to know things with my mind, of how much I try to explain the things I know with my heart. Instead of simply moving in harmony I reach for reasons to justify what I know is right. All the "Man" things that were active in my life now felt like anchors and limitations. I also recognized how firmly I still cling to them.

TURKEY

I had taken a break. I sat rolling over in my mind the dynamics currently in my life. I was thinking about things I felt I needed to do, of how I must budget my time and money to balance the obligations in my life and feeling very stressed. Suddenly the essence of Turkey stood before me. I was surprised by his appearance and the feeling of him. There was a dignity to him that I had not suspected.

"You have lived with my energy most of your life. You give away easily but I do not think you understand either the power of giveaway or the potential destruction of it.

"Man tends to see giveaway either as a something for nothing situation, or a gift with strings.

"Giveaway is part of the way of things. All food is a gift—rain, light, air—even life itself is a gift. They are not gifts you must earn. However, they are gifts to be respected and acknowledged. The power of giveaway is in knowing that everything

you have is a gift and that giving is a natural part of the movement of life. Nothing truly belongs to you alone. There is power in giveaway because you move in harmony with the way of things and demonstrate respect.

"The potential destruction of it can be seen when man uses giveaway as payment for wrongs, or as an investment in something they expect in return. Or, when he begins to give his personal power away.

"Part of the gift of life is choice in any situation. All thoughts, feelings and actions are choice and to give away the power of that choice diminishes you.

"Giveaway with understanding and respect increases your being and adds to the harmony of things. Giveaway with the wrong energy or reasons decreases you.

"Look honestly at what you are giving and why you are giving it. If there is peace in the action then you move in harmony. If there is any other feeling then you are moving in disharmony"

And I understood why Turkey had chosen to speak. I began to see some of the dynamics I had been struggling with from a different perspective.

GRASSHOPPER

I was gathering herbs in a field. Hundreds of grasshoppers jumped around me as I moved. I noticed that there was a playfulness about it rather than fear, and I enjoyed the game with them.

I thought no more about it until I was back home carrying the herbs into the house. A large grasshopper sat on my porch and did not move even though I passed him several times.

Finally I stopped and asked him if there were something on his mind.

"Do you know anything we are good for?"

Without really thinking I said, "My cat likes to eat grasshoppers."

Immediately I felt I had put my foot in it. However, to my surprise, the grasshopper laughed.

"Have you watched your cat hunt us? There is pure enjoyment in the process. That is all we know.

"Joy in being and absolute freedom are the gifts we have to offer.

"We never know where we will land when we launch ourselves into the air. And we use any excuse to take off. There is delight in not knowing where each jump will take us or what we will find when we land. We meet whatever challenge we land in and then leap to another.

"It is the process that is fun—it doesn't matter what the outcome is, just doing it is enough.

"Man never knows what the next five minutes will bring him either. He can choose to have delight in this or heavily try to create the illusion that he is in control.

"There is total freedom in accepting the not knowing, and total joy in not having it matter."

I would like to feel that way about life. Still, as I begin to try thinking in that direction, I hear all kinds of inner admonitions: "That's irresponsible, if you really lived that way you would accomplish nothing, you would be useless. You must do something worthwhile with your life, not just fritter it away."

Would I feel as if I were negligent, wasteful and a "bad" person if I enjoyed the process? How can feeling free and joyful and full of enthusiasm anticipating the next surprise be a bad thing?

I certainly have some mixed up values!

41

MORE DOLPHIN

Animals. They travel with me often now, reminding me that I may be a "two-legged" but I am still one of them—that to be in touch with my "animal nature" does not mean something negative or crude. Somehow man has decided that he is not animal and in the process lost touch with his own being. There have been various attempts to restore the connection. However, the number of words it takes to communicate such simple things is an indication of how far we've grown away from our true selves.

In the midst of the complex patterns of confusion around us, the effort to reestablish that simplicity within ourselves feels almost overwhelming at times. We not only contend with what is around us, we have conflict within us that further muddies the issue. I can appreciate the desire to retreat from all signs of civilization. I would like to just focus on resolving my own conflicts. But, I must "be" in the emotional chaotic sea around me and attempt to "be" as clear as possible—sometimes it seems more than I can do.

Dolphin, I could use a breath of air.

Their response whispered in my ear. *"Reach for it. It can be found in things around you. The stones you wear, the trees you see. You are deep in the sea right now, you must find air giving things around you for survival. Even the smallest air-giving thing can help you reach the next one, until you can find the surface.*

"When your being is air-hungry your mind can become poisoned and it is no longer clear. Reach, let your mind touch air-giving things and breathe with them. The sadness of a poisoned mind pulls you deeper in the sea and the pressure increases the deeper you go."

The stones in my necklace, a tree in the wind, a flying bird, and the sky with deep blue and clouds moving. Amazing! It works! Even reading what I've written does not feel as heavy as it did when I was writing it. And I remember now how I used to get through the stifling days of my childhood by reaching out to nature's life giving strength and "breathing" it in with my heart.

MOCKINGBIRD

People of many paths come to our door. Each of them wants to talk about "their way," and seem to expect me to agree with it. After a day spent talking to several of them, one after another, recognizing valid points in what they said as well as weaknesses in their constructs, I sat quietly attempting to find a balance within myself. I began to seek my inner being to get in touch with who I was after all the different energies and ideas were exchanged. I felt as though I had been out in a high wind that kept changing direction. I had trouble focusing because a bird singing outside my window kept cutting through my concentration. Finally I gave up and listened. It was then that the songs began stimulating words in my head.

"I am mockingbird. You know me. You've listened to me for hours on summer nights. Have you heard only the notes?

"I've told you over and over—each bird has a song of its own. The song comes from its heart and soul, expressing the music of its being. Many of them forget their songs for a while and only squawk, for each bird thinks its own song is the only song worth singing. Yet even in their squawking there are notes of their song. And each song has a life and charm of its own.

44

"There is beauty in all their songs and I find all of them worth singing.

"Find the beauty of each song and appreciate it. You need sing only the notes you find personally appealing. But do not reject any music that is clear and sweet, for there is richness in all songs of the soul no matter how the notes are put together. And, all music is composed of the same stuff. Seek the richness and clarity in what you hear and create your own song from the combinations that feel beautiful to you and you will find nourishment in the music—no matter how it is sung."

Inner balance no longer seemed to be a problem.

DOVE

After a full day of business, I decided to go ahead and drive home. I knew it wasn't a wise decision. It would be long and difficult, but I wanted to be home and felt I could handle it. On the way I encountered hail the size of lemons that cracked the windshield, lightning that was striking all around me and winds that pushed the car around on the road. There was no place to stop, I was in the "middle of nowhere" and an inner voice kept telling me to keep moving even though my fear wanted to stop and find someplace to hide. I later discovered this was the edge of a tornado that had passed through where I was driving.

When I stopped for gas I realized I was rather shaken by the ordeal, but I called on my endurance and stubbornly went on. I did not realize until the next day that I was in a mild state of shock. I tried to understand what was going on, but my entire level of function was screaming "TILT." It was a friend who brought up the subject of doves and how they go into shock if their feathers are ruffled the wrong way and can die from it with no mark on them.

I was still having trouble putting things into perspective a day or so later, so I called on the dove to see if she could help me at least understand what was going on internally—there seemed to be more than just a physical problem.

Dove responded, *"We are beings of gentleness and love. In our strength, we can reach out and touch your heart. Violence is not our way. Yet, we must accept it as a part of the way of things. Some of us handle it better than others.*

46

Gentleness and love are not weaknesses. They both have incredible power of their own. However, if we remove the strength of them by focusing on fear, we have little to draw on.

"You have been working with dove energy and you slipped to the contrary side. You were in a threatening situation where you felt out of control, felt fear, and fell into a 'victim' state of mind, helpless against the elements that spoke of death. This was not a matter of dealing with death, it was a matter of dealing with the feeling of being a victim, helplessness and the loss of hope. You had no influence over what was happening, you could do nothing to either change it, stop it, or protect yourself once it had begun.

"It is an old fear, one that man has carried from the beginning. There were things that could have been done to prevent the problem if you had allowed yourself to be aware and listen to more than just what your ego wanted. This is part of the guilt that goes along with this state of mind. Shift to the side of strength within yourself. It is not the fact of having no control that is the problem. No one ever has control. Control outside yourself is an illusion. It is the victim state of mind that creates the shock and damage. Allow yourself to know the side of strength. Let go of the fear. Fear accomplishes nothing except paralyzing your action and dissolving the power you have.

"We know both sides. We can help you shift the energy so you can feel the difference."

I felt a sudden, dramatic change within me. My energy was back, and the feeling of confusion was gone. Only then did I fully recognize the fear I'd had, because it was now gone too, and with it, other victimized feelings I'd been carrying. I felt more like me than I had for quite a while. I also had a greater understanding of what victim consciousness is, as well as its effects.

BLUE HERON

I am in Houston. I have an appointment to meet someone and I am early, so I sit in the car. A storm is whipping the trees, and there is a cold rain.

Water birds come to mind. Blue Heron (neighbors at home) touches me gently with her feathers.

"There is power in the storm, a clean power, a cleansing power. We draw from water and wind, all 'water birds' do.

"Water and wind cleanse the air and feed the earth. We use the power to work with spirit and being.

"Let our feathers gently clear your mind of 'pollution.'

"Let our medicine restore your spirit.

"Fly with it.

"Move with joy.

"When you are heavy with man things, call on us

"Allow us to touch you and remind you what it means to fly and how it feels to be cool and clean inside."

As I sat in the car feeling the touch of the Heron moving through my being, the mundane irritations and tension began to dissolve. I began to feel as though I could face anything, handle anything, and remain clearly in the flow of the universe.

SPIDER AGAIN

I sit struggling with an inner monster of the past, realizing how deep the roots are and how far back it goes—how extensive the effects are in ways I deal with the world. I begin to understand why many of the attempts at coping with those effects and the desire to change them have had little real effect. I have not understood before what I was dealing with. This is nothing simple. This IS a major undertaking. Perhaps the major undertaking of my life.

As I sit gathering forces to begin dealing with what my recent self-honesty has revealed, I hear a sound.

Turning to identify it I find a wasp caught in a spider web and a spider half the size of the wasp attempting to overcome this deadly enemy in its web. Spider essence gently touches my shoulder and speaks in my ear.

"Watch, my dear. See how she does this. Learn and understand."

And I spent the next hour watching and learning.

The spider stayed well back observing, and threw a line attaching it to the wasp then ran around to another vantage point and threw another. She appeared to loop it when she could, then going back and strengthening her web, attaching her lines, anchoring them more securely and then going back to observe the problem of the wasp and pick another place to throw another line. She went through these maneuvers again and again—stopping, waiting, checking, throwing a line and again watching, adjusting, moving and trying again. None of it seemed to have any effect at all. Still she kept at it. The threads seemed to have no strength, the wasp broke most of them. There was no apparent progress either way. The wasp was still caught, and it looked as though the spider was no closer to conquering her enemy.

Then, she seemed to sense something I did not. Perhaps she could feel the wasp tiring, or she felt she had the wasp secure enough, or she had a new idea of how to approach the situation. After observing this time, she moved in to an area close to the wasp and quickly looped a line and moved away, pulling it tight. Then after observing, she moved in where she could attempt a bite, the edge of a wing, or a leg, then move, throw a line, be still, adjust, tighten, strengthen and move again.

Another spider came and tried to move in on her kill, distracting her. If the first spider missed and the wasp killed her off, the other spider could have two free meals. The first spider kept watching and protected her work as she continued. Slowly, almost imperceptibly the tide of the battle shifted, and still she kept up the pattern. Little by little I could see her overcoming the wasp until finally it was still. Even then she let it lie for a while before wrapping the wasp thoroughly and carrying it away to consume the deadly enemy at her leisure.

Spider then spoke again:

"This is how you deal with your monster. Determination is the key, and holding the goal clearly in your mind. Never forget the poison of your adversary, but do not let the seeming power of your monster disarm you. You have the ability to win if you keep the battle on your terms. Stay within your power and keep at it."

Sometimes a demonstration can make a few words contain more sense than hours of lectures.

HAWK

Animals keep popping into my mind with bits of consciousness. Sometimes I will see an animal do something and their spirit mind links briefly with mine and I hear them speak, telling me to notice what I see, there is meaning here.

Such as seeing a hawk intent on its prey in a high wind, not moving from its position, it said, *"See, it is possible to go against the currents if you are determined enough. By narrowing your focus and keeping your mind on one idea, you can fight the wind and hang onto your position. You may even catch whatever you are after. But the process uses so much energy that you lose more than you gain."*

Oh yes! I see so many people doing that!

I, of course, would never be that foolish!

DEER

Deer fills my head. I feel the weight of antlers. It is the eyes that are riveting, I seem to see them and at the same time see out of them while waves of feelings flow through me:

Clarity.

Gentleness.

Strength.

Serenity.

"We know. We are prey. It is part of our purpose. But we are not victims. We are able to protect our own, and flourish among predators. We see. More than see, we know with all our being the beauty around us. We know how to play. We rejoice in the pleasures of our lives, even the small ones like finding a choice leaf. We sense far more than man realizes. His inner chaos is heavy for us so we tend to avoid him. With our senses we know when we are marked and it is our time. We still go through the action of flight and resistance.

"Acceptance does not mean 'quit trying.' Continuing effort to improve things as we see them is harmonious with the way of things. Acceptance has more to do with

releasing expectations and demands, and recognizing that there are greater aspects in the design we do not understand. Even within acceptance it is in harmony to resist. The outcome still may not be what we want it to be, but it will be in harmony.

"Honest effort in our own behalf is always appropriate. Change, after all, is a fundamental part of the way of things. No matter what seems to be, change is in harmony and always possible.

"Rejoice in all, and continue to move."

This is what the essence of heroism is all about!

Being a Life Master does not mean having everything go the way you want it to. We are here to do, patterned by what we think, and learn in the process. We are allowed to try for what we want, but we don't demand it, or expect it if we are to fulfill our purpose.

BUTTERFLY

I turned onto the dirt road leading to my house. The summer had been dry and the sun coming through the trees made rays in the dust. I drove slowly and somewhat mindlessly, absorbing the ruralness I enjoy so much. A butterfly flew in the window and brought me into focus by landing on my head. I then noticed that the road was extraordinarily full of butterflies and I began to drive more carefully to avoid hitting them. Still, the butterfly stayed on my head gently fanning my face with the opening and closing of its wings.

"See how light they are? They float more than fly.

"You have found it remarkable how few butterflies are hit or damaged as you go down the road.

"Do you understand the power of gentleness?

"Observe. It is the lightness of their being that allows them to float on air currents and avoid damage.

"To accomplish this we had to change.

"We crawled before we saw our own truth.

"It is the heaviness of man's being that keeps him crawling. See your own truth and allow change to occur in your spirit. Allow the light gentleness of your be- ing to carry you on currents

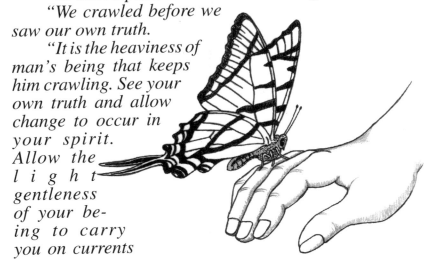

that avoid damage.

"Once you understand and avoid damage to yourself, you will not cause damage outside yourself either.

"It is simple really. The joy we are is a natural part of man as well."

Oh, dear butterfly, I feel what you mean. But such lightness seems so difficult in a world that glorifies heaviness. And it is in such a world that I must live. Help me with the changes necessary to become like you.

AND MORE
SPIDER

As transactions are occurring around me, the buzzing in my ear becomes a whisper:

"*Have you not noticed, my dear, how none of the patterns you are working on ever seem finished? It is man who seems to feel there are endings to things. Anything you think about or are involved in becomes continuous. It may change form, but nothing ends. The most complicated webs in existence are still constructed with a single thread.*"

Yes, I see the threads weaving before my eyes.

CHEETAH

I have always enjoyed animal films. So, when our local video store began stocking nature films I eagerly rented them. In one of the films they talked of how each Cheetah had the same genetic imprint.

I puzzled about this and tried to use logic to decipher how this could possibly happen. All my knowledge of genetics told me that this was not possible.

Then it occurred to me. All the creatures I had spoken with thus far had been familiar to me. They had been around all my life. But Cheetah has an animal spirit too. Why not call the spirit and ask? The following story is how the cheetah spirit responded:

"Once the cheetah lived in many parts of the world. Their numbers were great and their speed made them powerful. They began to feel they were much better than all the other animals because they were so fast. There were many differences among them. But, overall they were arrogant, demanding of attention and painfully intruded on many other animals' lives and territory. When the other animals tried to make them stop, the cheetah merely laughed and ran away. They felt they were special and could get away with whatever they

58

wanted to do. They became unmerciful pests, tormenting other animals and laughing at their distress and dismay.

The Great Spirit saw this and laid many lessons in their path, but they ignored the lessons. Instead they became more and more arrogant until their attitudes began affecting how they were with their own kind as well. They began fighting among themselves and no longer enjoyed the company of their own kind. Their numbers began to dwindle and their power faded.

There was concern over this and a council was called. The council lasted for many days and still there was arguing and fighting. Each one had ideas of what the problem was and each one arrogantly insisted that what he thought was right and that the others needed to follow his way to resolve the problems.

A jackal watched this for a while and began to laugh. The cheetahs turned their anger on him but the jackal only laughed.

Finally they said, "If you think you are so smart, then tell us what you think."

Jackal moved to where all could hear him and said, "It is obvious that there can be no agreement as long as you remain so involved with what each of you wants. You need to see further than the differences if you are to survive beyond this council."

The cheetahs despised the jackal, but could not deny the truth when it was so plainly put in front of them. Finally they had found something they could agree on. So they decided to join together in this one thing and gathered all their medicine to ask the Great Spirit to help them erase the differences between them so they could unite and regain their power. Their action was clear, but their request was not, for the true intent behind the action was that each one wanted the Great Spirit to change all the other cheetahs to suit himself.

The Great Spirit looked down and saw their medicine. He also saw how they used their prayers dishonestly, pretending they were asking for the good of all when each of them was really asking for the right to go on selfishly doing exactly as he pleased, having no respect for anything.

Great Spirit spoke, "Since you do not respect differences and you do not honor the abilities you have; since you do not value My creation and you do not see that all ways have their place in the balance of things, I will give you what you ask and make you all exactly alike."

And they became as the Great Spirit decreed. They are all alike, as though they all came from the same mother, from the same seed.

It is true they no longer disagree, for the weaknesses one has, they all have. What frightens one, frightens them all. What harms one, harms all. They now understand the basic sameness that links everything.

However, they also understand that differences give the strength and power to grow and learn. They no longer have the differences to help each other cope with life and grow from their experiences. They have stopped growing. Their wisdom is deeper now, although sameness has locked them into a narrow way of being. Even so, they too have purpose, for they have become an example to others to avoid such arrogance and to respect differences.

If man does not begin to appreciate differences instead of defining anything different as bad will we become as the Cheetah?

We must respect "otherness" in order to survive. No person can possibly see everything. We need separate viewpoints to understand the whole! After all, the whole includes "other" as well.

OWL

I can't sleep. I've been trying for four hours. No apparent problem, just no sleep. So I decide to go outside and enjoy the summer night.

Owl slips into my mind with a soft stirring of wings, but he is silent—the silent hunter of the night. The seer, looking clearly into dark places, stirring old things—fears and shadowed feelings that run deep. Do you have something to teach, or are you merely hunting?

Self doubt. Questions unanswered. The old displaced feelings of belonging nowhere all become active as I sit here waiting and wondering.

Then Owl spoke. *"The dark places will always be a part of you. Seeing them will help you understand. Knowing them for what they are will help you avoid slipping into the world of shadow.*

"However, seeing, knowing and understanding will not bring them out of the dark—dark is their nature.

Dark is what they are, and must be to keep the balance within.

"It is your choice whether to give them power or not.

"Let your eyes adjust to the darkness and look into your own dark places. By allowing yourself to see, you give yourself the choice. Seeing can seem painful, but it is only the dark defending its right to rule (which you have given it for a long time by denying it exists within you).

"The power of dark things within is strong in man—strong and active until it is seen and choices are made—and still the dark within will try many tricks to stay in control.

"Man is an abusive, disrespectful be-ing until darkness is seen and the choice is NOT.

Stop giving self reasons, excuses, and justifications not to see. Acknowledge what is within you and simply choose NOT. It seems such a simple choice and yet man finds all kinds of ways to let inner darkness have control.

"Fear, doubt, pain, punishment— each of you heap so much of these dark things on yourselves that you naturally ac-cept them from other sources.

"See into your darkness.

"Know it for what it is.

"And stop giving it power."

It does seem simple. Yet in practice I see so many ways I continue abusing myself in my mind. I also begin to see how that self abuse sets up a mental pattern that ac-cepts and participates in abusive, disre-spectful patterns in everyday life. It seems too simple just to stop. Yet, if I acknowledge my power to change, then the power is there to do just that—stop.

I can be whatever kind of person I choose to be, if I am willing to look honestly into my own dark corners and do something about what I find.

EAGLE

I sit weighted down with the feeling of real and potential problems. I have heard from many animals who speak so clearly and simply about life and living and I wonder how to apply their lessons in Man's world, where bills are to be paid, and responsibilities are to be met.

I feel surrounded by the destruction of their simplicity. Our dishonesty with self, the dishonoring of our world, and—Eagle!

I feel Eagle!

There is a fog in my inner hearing, but I feel Eagle.

Then I hear harrier, the messenger, cry in my ear.

And the majesty of Eagle circles closer. First a feeling of calm, neutral strength flows over me, a gentle smile.

"I see it all.

"I fly to silent heights man seldom reaches. There is so much that Man misses by crawling on the ground. He sees so little that it is easy for him to get lost in illusion.

"Pieces of truth are only pieces, and in his attempt to see the whole, man fills in the gaps for himself.

"You all think too much.

"You try to figure things out instead of allowing yourselves to know.

"You believe you can think

64

your way out of anything—that your intellect is your magic.

"You think that emotion is the same as feeling.

"Your heart knows a great deal. But knowing is a quiet thing and the noise of your thinking drowns it out.

"Fly with me and see further than your thoughts."

"Now?" I ask.

"Now," he answers.

We soar to a plane where I have no words—only feeling. I start trying to describe it to myself.

"No, don't get lost in the words... stay with me."

"How can I share this without them?"

"Know!"

And, I know!

Clarity...

Sureness...

Silence...

Softly, I return. Reluctantly I am again in my chair, feeling that I am part of something. Something beyond expressing in words. There is peace in being a part of this something, a balance that I feel can sustain me through anything, if I can stay in touch with it.

I thank the Eagle, even though he is already gone, and wonder if it is possible for words to communicate this.

THE MEANING

After about a year of opening myself to accept animal teaching so I could attempt to communicate what I had learned to others, I seemed no closer to their simple, direct clarity than when I started. Their truth has always touched me and shifted my perspective, but I never seemed to have that perspective on my own. I always felt their medicine working on me, yet they seemed in a different world. Their medicine was still magic to me. I felt frustrated because theirs was a wise world I wanted to understand and incorporate into my living.

Still, every time I reached for it I hit a barrier, a wall that felt impenetrable. I had tried many directions, many methods, and always I hit the same wall. I began to realize this was a barrier that I had created and I was the only one who could remove it and doubled my efforts.

Even though I felt that I chipped parts of it away, I still seemed no closer. I began to doubt that there was anything beyond the wall, that what others saw beyond it was not real. I felt enclosed, frustrated, cramped and extremely uncomfortable.

I called the medicine and asked for help. I was losing heart and needed to know there was something beyond the wall.

The response was overwhelming, it was as though many animals converged, touching me and lifting me and filling me with quiet gentleness, soothing the anxiousness. Then they showed me an egg.

At first it had no meaning, then I realized that I was beyond my wall, looking back.

They said, *"Yes, you have been growing inside.*

That's why you are so uncomfortable. You have only to break the shell to become the person you can be.

"Discomfort is a natural part of the growth. Do not be impatient, there is a maturing process going on, and there is timing involved. You will not break free of the shell until the time is appropriate.

"You have been living on the food provided within the shell. You are running out of that food, it no longer sustains you—that is part of your discomfort.

"The shell can only be broken from the inside and when you are cramped enough and hungry enough you will break it. You will know how, and you will do it when the time is right."

"I want out," I said.

"When the time is right and you truly want out you will know what needs to be done."

The image gave me some comfort and helped me to continue my efforts even though the frustration and anxiety continued to grow. Then came the sinking feeling of what composed the barrier. I did not really want out, I only wanted the discomfort to cease. I still wanted to do things in the same old ways, see things as I always had and feel I controlled the world around me in the context that I had accepted and these things were not past, they were present, current and active. The wall was all based on dishonesty, and I was trying to fit reality inside the shell where I could manipulate it to suit what I had thought I wanted. Unfortunately, what I had thought I wanted was also based on not being honest with myself.

If I broke the shell and really started being honest with myself and the world, EVERYTHING would change!

To lose all I think I know for a complete unknown— talk about frightening!

To give up the control I felt I had, to give up all I believe I had a grasp on, to let go of my entire world, to know nothing and start from scratch, I could not pretend to do this. I could not do it to please anyone outside myself. I could not fake or con or lie to myself about it or the shell would remain.

This is what it means to be reborn!

Then the grasshopper touched me, *"It is OK to know nothing."*

Dolphin said, *"You need to feed more than your body."*

Mouse said, *"If you do not go back to your natural way of being, your life will be wasted."*

Turtle said, *"A shell is a poor defense."*

Rabbit said, *"Fear brings only death."*

Turkey said, *"You are giving away your right to be if the shell remains."*

Dove said, *"Would you choose to stay a victim?"*

Hawk said, *"Would you fight against your own currents?"*

Deer said, *"Change, after all, is the fundamental way of things."*

Cheetah said, *"Would you choose arrogance and disrespect?"*

Owl said, *"Do you wish to let your shadows continue to rule you?"*

Eagle said, *"You've seen there is more. Is what you have really so much?"*

Mockingbird said, *"You must be able to hear other songs to find your own."*

Squirrel said, *"You take all this too seriously."*

Blue Heron said, *"Think what your spirit can feel like—cool and clean."*

Butterfly said, *"It is only your spirit changing form."*

Bat said, *"Remember!"*

Snake said, *"It is only the shedding of old skins you have outgrown and no longer need."*

Buzzard said, *"You only think it is painful at the time."*

Ant said, *"Be patient with yourself, you do not have to demand perfection all at once."*

Spider said, *"Just begin breaking the shell, my dear, one thought at a time, one day at a time. Stop lying to yourself and the pattern will change. It has already begun to change."*

And who was I really then? What was I? Who and what would I be?

Whatever it was, it would be more real. And I began to feel, rather than hear, a cracking sound.

PART 2
EARTH CHILD

BREAKING
THE SHELL

As I was concluding the first part of this book, I thought I was finished. Everything had come full circle, all statements were whole and complete, and it seemed that the concentration of animal teachings had completed their purpose.

Not so.

After a year of being taught by animals and making many painful personal discoveries, the boundaries enclosing my world began to feel different. Still, there was no sudden change in my life and being. There were those around me who saw no change at all. But, how I saw the world and how I saw myself began to shift. I began to see many weaknesses in the way I functioned and I made efforts to change. This was frustrating because each time I thought I had made some grand strides I would look again and find I had only modified my old patterns to convince myself how much I had changed.

Stress factors in my life seemed to peak, but after entering a sweat lodge and uttering the prayer, "Help me recognize my own truth and to find the courage to act on it that I might function more appropriately," everything hit the fan.

I experienced periods of panic and severe anxiety in the process. There was a frantic stretching, pounding, internal breaking, and floods of honesty I would have been much more comfortable without. I began to see how distorted my life had been, how my existence was foreign to my nature, how abusive I had always been to myself in my own mind, how destructive, how restrictive, and how this had been reflected outwardly to those around me. I began to realize the extent I had been self-centered around a constructed being that had nothing to do with my personal inner truth. It became painfully clear that with each ugly "thing" I discovered, and forcefully determined I would discard, there were parts of me clinging desperately to the many shards of illusions associated with it.

The medicine people of my "family" remained supportive and continued telling me this was all right, this was a kind of death that was needed to move beyond myself into being. This helped me accept the process, but the inner chaos continued.

SNAKE AGAIN

And snake appears...
"You have forgotten me. I can help you, you know.
Of course, help me shed these clinging old skins.

"Abrasiveness helps to clear them, but harshness only cuts the new skin and each place it bleeds robs you of energy needed for the process.

"You are ridding yourself of the old skin and the new skin is not toughened yet. Each part of the new skin cannot be fully formed until the old is cleared away. Until then it is very sensitive and needs a little time to adjust.

"Be gentle with yourself.

"Remember, a chick is very weak and wobbly when it first leaves the shell and a fawn can barely stand when first born."

Yes, I must firmly stumble forth and be tolerant of my weakness and confusion.

Yes, patterns need to change, but I also need to remember that these patterns are not really outside myself, they are my creation, mine to claim and mine to change from within.

A part of me understood this, and a part of me kept trying to see things as being outside myself, and trying to make other people or things be responsible instead of me.

FLY

Flies would not leave me alone. At first I was annoyed because they kept crawling on my face... then I realized that they too wanted me to listen.

"We too fly. Our very name has the power of flight.

"We are born out of garbage, excrement and death. We crawl a bit, transform, and fly.

"Man turns away from such things and when his own garbage, excrement and death begin to pile up, he tries to cover it. He pretends it doesn't exist, or tells himself and the world that it is not his own, it is what is around him. All this does is create more dishonesty, more distance from his own reality.

"Claim what is yours, appreciate it. It is a part of you and you can grow beyond it just as we do. You will crawl a bit at first, then the acceptance and growing wisdom will allow you to transform, and when you actively choose to change—you too will fly."

I have seen some of those ugly things in myself. But to claim them... to appreciate them? In my mind, I know that I must accept them as part of myself before I can change them, because I cannot change things that are not mine. But when I encounter any of them, I still recoil at the very thought! I don't want to admit that anything like that is a part of me... I want to reject the whole idea!

BEAR

As time passed I grew to understand how the animals are another aspect of my medicine family—perhaps the only true medicine family I have because they are completely neutral as no human understands how to be. Humans have investment in the outcome of all interactions and our efforts are affected by our expectations, or our desires. The only possible way we can function with true clarity is if we get out of our own way—no ego, no emotions, no investment in the outcome—nothing "personal" involved.

But, at the same time we need to be totally involved, aware, and paying attention to what is going on around and within ourselves.

I began to realize that I really did not pay much attention to anything unless I expected to "get" something from the situation. The extent of my self- centeredness and my efforts expended to "create" what I wanted from each situation kept slapping me in the face. I looked around and saw that this was how people generally dealt with life. It was a part of the culture around me. Somehow, that did little to comfort me in my own realizations. "Normal" doesn't make something right.

My almost constant involvement in drama and the attempt to gain attention at all costs became so obvious that I grew sick of my own company. And quieting these things in my mind left me frightened and ignorant of how to be. I began to wonder just how disgusted I could get with myself.

Then the extent of my distortions began to dawn. How could I give up failing when it was the only thing I felt I knew how to do really well? All the drama of how pitifully I was struggling and having such a difficult time succeeding was simply part of the game. I did not want to give up the pleasure of playing that game. It was an integral part of what I thought I was! All my ideas of personal value were tied up in playing that game that told me in order to succeed I had to fail. It wasn't even my own game! I had inherited the rules, accepted them as truth, and made them a part of me or what I had chosen to be.

This "ugly being" I was beginning to see was me— as I was, had chosen to be, as I am until I do something to change it and make it different. All the illusions and beliefs and self-convincing little lies in the world do not make the reality of truth any different. I could only pretend to be the character in a movie or book or some composite I had created in my mind. Without the reality of action that backed it up it was all an internal fantasy.

I felt overwhelmed. There was so much around me that fed into all the aspects I wanted to change. I could not change the world outside me, and I felt caught in systems beyond my control. Game or not, it seemed all my efforts led nowhere.

Bear loomed before me, large.

"We are strong. There is not much that can overcome us. Yet when winter comes and there are difficult times, with little food and harshness all around, we

hibernate. We sleep and wait for the difficult times to be over.

"Man is obsessed with taking action when things get difficult. He struggles to change the situation. Even in our strength, can we change winter? There are times when we must merely wait for a shift in energies, wait for things to unfold before anything can change.

"Yes, we all do what we can, do what we must in difficult times. Action may need to continue, but your action will not change winter. You simply do what you can to get through it. Winter will take its natural course and pass when its own timing says it is appropriate. Only then will your action be fruitful.

"And, always know that another winter will come in the natural cycle of things and some winters will be harsher than others.

"Struggle if you must, but know where your struggles take you. Recognize what you must do, and do not waste energies in trying to change winter. These things are not punishments, they are not aimed at man or animal. It is just the way of things.

"Man gets lost in the idea that he has control. He feels he must be able to master everything and if winter comes it must be someone's fault. He forgets there are things he will never control. All he ever has hope of controlling is himself, and then only if he understands the realities of himself and the way of things."

Yes, I must allow life to evolve naturally and stop "pushing the river."

Will my efforts cease if change does not happen according to my time schedule? Will my commitment run out by a certain date? Am I afraid I will not follow through if it is not accomplished quickly?

Maybe I just do not trust my own level of commitment.

Ah! I recognize another aspect of the game: successful failure to complete the project! In focusing on battles I can arrange an overall loss of the war that a part of me does not want to win.

Relax! Trust my own commitment and keep working on the follow-through. It is really only my own will operating here, and I will follow the course I set for myself, changing only as I choose to take action.

I could use some help formulating a plan of action in this war with myself. How can I begin approaching my own deceptions without being deceived?

BADGER

The pointed nose touched mine, sending currents of shock through my system in my inward journey. Bright intelligent eyes glittered close to mine and the stripes along its head of dark and light seemed to provide a mirror image of my strangely graying hair.

As it climbed on my shoulder and began its message I could feel it chuckling at the good joke of how it had gotten my attention.

"If there is one word that belongs to badger, it is tenacity. We hang on beyond all reason.

"Yes, we are a strong teacher of the use of roots and plants. Our digging allows us to know them well. But that is almost incidental in what we have to teach.

"We do not give you our trust easily. We are shy and careful. To gain that trust, you must earn it. However, once you have earned our love and trust, you have it forever. Take a lesson from that and allow time to test the value of something before you devote your loyalty to anyone or anything, and you will have a solid base.

"We are not aggressive. We do not attack randomly. We are like most natural creatures. Normally you would not know we exist, even when we live right under your nose. But if we are threatened or are engaged in battle for any reason, we fight savagely and will not quit until we win or die. We will take on any-thing,

no matter what its size or capabilities, if we feel we have reason. In seeking stories of badgers, you will find we have driven off bears and other animals you would think impossible for us to succeed against.

"We are busy, constantly working on something. But we love to play as well. We know that humor is something that makes all activity light, even when it is intense.

"If we trust you enough to be a friend, our companionship and humor can enrich your life, but we will never be a "pet." We value our independence too highly, so any attempt to confine us would be considered a betrayal of trust.

"All these things we have to share. However, the true medicine power we can teach you is that of opening new ways. We go into the earth and use our claws to make pathways where none existed before and expose the roots of medicine so they are accessible. In the process, we bring things that have been hidden into the light.

"This we joyfully do as part of our everyday chores. Chores you might find boring and tedious if you did not see beneath the surface as we do.

"Let me share my understanding with you and help you open new ways for yourself, finding joy in the process."

Yes, badger, help me find new ways of being. Help me look beneath the surface of things, and bring things that have been hidden into the light.

RATTLESNAKE

As I drive to Nashville, through the mountains, autumn colors have just begun. There is a feeling of joy and subtle excitement. It is a time of change and the seasons remind me this is natural and beautiful. A feeling of power and impending "something" comes over me. By now I recognize it is an animal wishing to communicate, so I allow its guidance to take me off the interstate to a place in the mountains. I stop, and settle down to smoke with the animal.

The air becomes like a Renoir painting as the metal of the car seems to dissolve from around me and I find on the ground before me an enormous rattlesnake—a diamond back with soft black markings that are vividly clear. It is within two feet of me, coiled, and my reaction is instant caution.

"Sit down and trust."

Slowly, I settle on the ground, sitting cross legged in front of the rattler—not without some question of my sanity even though a part of me knows this is a vision.

"I am snake. You know of our connection with the earth as well as our wisdom of shedding skins. You have asked for our guidance so I will now tell you more of the wisdom of our particular kind.

"I hold enough poison to bring down a horse. My poison would cause a lingering painful death. We have this power. Yet, when one of our kind bit your dog, she only had a day of discomfort and was then fine.

"We have learned to control our poison. We can bite and inject

83

nothing if we choose to.

"There are many of us, yet how often do you hear of anyone being bitten or dying from one of our bites? We avoid being harmful if we can.

"We use our poison only if there is purpose... mainly for feeding ourselves.

"Even when startled, trapped, or teased (as your dog was doing) we will use judgment as to whether the poison is appropriate or not, and how much to use.

"We have learned the ways of peace.

"Man is full of poison too. His bite can be as deadly as ours. The only difference is that our poison comes from fangs, yours comes from words. You have the same power within you as we do and you hold it in your mouth.

"Do you bite and poison from need or want is the question. Have you learned to withhold the poison when it is not necessary? Many times, even in threatening situations, a poisonless bite is all that is needed to keep balance.

"Man tends to bite and throw all his poison out of fear—his anger, his righteousness, his sense of urgency to 'correct' things are all based in fear. They are excuses to make it all right to inject poison and cause lingering, painful deaths. However, these excuses are only wants with their foundations in fear.

"Look at your ways. See the poison you have put into the world around you and ask yourself honestly, is this needed, or can I deal with it more gently?

"In learning this balance of power, you may get stepped on a few times, but you will live, and in the process you will learn when to avoid, when to bite and how much poison is truly required.

"Examine each instance. Learn from each move, and you will develop the wisdom of rattlesnake."

I begin to see how much damage I have done with ill chosen words! I also see that the damage has come more from my own fears than any real threats.

You are right! It is important that I pay more attention to what I am saying, and how I am saying it. In that process I think it would be a good idea to begin examining WHY I am saying it as well!

ROBIN

On the surface, I was collecting tab tops as part of an effort to help a dialysis patient in Tulsa, a noble, acceptable thing to do. As I was diligently adding to my collection it dawned on me that I was really searching for myself, using this as an excuse to be out in nature and touch the earth.

I realized I have spent a great deal of my life involved in this sort of activity. In looking through my past, some of the more meaningful time I have spent has been searching—for cans, rocks, herbs, lead in the sand pits where my father used to go shooting. The process had always seemed more significant than finding the

objectives I had set.

Always, I think, I was really searching for myself even though the focus tended to be more on whatever excuse I had given myself to be out in nature. Whatever I was "finding" had no real meaning for me because so much of the time I was hiding what I was really searching for. However, it established a pattern that I struggle with now by placing more value in the set objective than what I am truly searching for.

A Robin hopped near me, fixed me with its stare as robins do, and said, *"Spring is near."*

I laughed, "Sure, but your timing is a bit off, this is barely February."

The bird moved closer, *"Spring is near! The blossoming forth of life that has seemed dead, but only slept for a while."*

It hopped even closer. *"Remember?*

"Remember me? I was the first bird you knew... I was an integral part of when you were becoming aware of the life within you.

"You have slept for a long time

"What you seek is found in the child who knew me."

I thought of the frightened child I had touched inside myself, finding only the same fears and pain I lived with now. In spite of all the grandiose ideas I had of myself, the truth was that I was still only a frightened little girl inside.

But Robin hopped impatiently and said, *"That child knew more than this. She held sunshine in her hands and joy in her heart. Find this part of her—you have only found the reasons you threw her away.*

"You find life in the earth and in nature. You go there to meet it and draw from it. You have not been allowing yourself the honesty of reaching for it. You always had to cover your need with excuses, to explain it with some purpose that would be accepted. And in that process you missed most of the reasons you went in the first place.

"You have begun to allow yourself direct gifts— this

is another step. Acknowledge your need for touching life around you and accept what you have really come for. Allow yourself the gift of finding and drawing life into your being through your connection with Nature. Allow yourself to let your life force flow into the generous life around you, rebuilding the natural cyclic flow of spirit where it will not be taken advantage of, where it is safe to remember."

As I touched the Robin spirit, I felt my breast swell, full of old pain, and turn orange under my covering of gray.

I felt the robin's encouraging support as it spoke again. *"Release the child from its prison. Value the natural part of yourself found in the child. That was always the real gift you denied yourself. This is the call of nature...............*

"Remember!

"As long as Man denies his natural self he will continue to destroy nature around him just as he attempts to destroy it within."

Nature still lives within me! My natural being is not dead, it has merely been ignored, and covered up. I have said it was not useful, or valuable, but it has not died and only waits for me to acknowledge it again.

FLY AGAIN

While traveling, I stopped at a restaurant to eat. I sat in the car, not wanting to move. My energy was low and I was wondering how I was going to go on with my business. I felt immobile.

A fly flew in the window into my face and then settled next to me in the sun. OK, what are you trying to tell me?

"I keep reminding you, as you crawl in your refuse, to fly.

"You cannot fly when you are heavy. Have you not noticed how often flies clean themselves and reorder their energies? Consciously clear the air and your energy often. Whenever you become more 'alive' and aware as you have been doing, you are more easily affected by all sorts of things. Even after you develop more firmness in your being you must be as conscious of this as we are. Constant alertness is what keeps us alive. Be ready to move when there is the slightest sign and consciously keep yourself as clear as you possibly can."

And the fly flew out of the window.

I reached for the smudge and filled the car with the sweet, clearing smell and immediately felt better. I resolved to be more aware and not to let myself get into this kind of slump again.

WOLF

People! Their attitudes and actions are so maddening and confusing. Am I this frustrating to others? I feel so bad when I lash out at them and add to the problems, but I also feel bad if I say nothing. Should I withdraw and separate myself from people altogether until I get this whole thing more sorted out?

Wolf nudges me with his nose.

"I have come to speak to you of the pack.

"You would call it family—not necessarily connected by blood ties but by understanding of needs.

"There is need to share, to give and receive caring. There is need for others to help with different aspects of survival. There are needs to play, to help carry responsibilities, and for comfort in difficult times.

"To have the pack, there must be a surrender of will and a willingness to give. For each must simply do his part in the understanding of total need. Personalities differ, so we must remember to allow for this and accept what is.

"Leaders do not become so by imposing their will, or appealing to the others, or convincing the others how much better they are. They just naturally stand out and the others make them leaders by giving them the respect of that honor. Nothing is demanded or expected.

"It is our nature to hunt.

90

We hunt and kill disease, even in our own kind.

"It is not natural for us to hunt man, but man hunts us.

"Man hunts us out of fear, because man, even in his delusions, knows of his sickness, and feels threatened.

"If one of us exhibited the willfulness, self-centeredness and denial of need that man does, we would turn that one away from the pack.

"If one of us carried the anger, denial of true self, and destructiveness some of you do, and he refused to acknowledge his sickness, we would hunt that one down if necessary.

"You see, there is loving support in a pack. However, if in sickness the renegade refused to accept either his sickness or the support available, and turned on the pack destructively, there would be no other solution for us.

"Is it truly so difficult for man to honor each other? Is it really so hard for man to acknowledge his need for his own kind? Is it such an effort to recognize his connection with all life around him? Is this arrogance truly a part of man or is it part of his insanity?

"Obviously, in our ability to see sickness we feel this to be insanity or we would not even bother trying to speak to you. However, this insanity grows to the level of sickness.

"If man does not open his heart and allow himself a pack, his sickness will grow beyond repair.

"There are forces more powerful than us to clear this great sickness.

"Man must give up his anger, his greed for power and control, and most of all, his fear if he is to survive.

"We continue to care even though you slaughter us. How can man not care for each other when so much caring is all around him? Man does unspeakable things to animals, but that is nothing compared to what he does to his own kind, and to himself.

"There need not be any guilt over this. Just open

your heart, acknowledge your pack, and stop."

To acknowledge the pack, we must connect with all life.

To do that we must stop fearing life itself.

Surprise! I find that I feel threatened by the idea! To give up fearing life means that I must trust it and that is truly scary!

BIG HORN SHEEP

I am driving over the mountain passes to Aspen. There is a new snow on the mountains and ice on the road. And Big Horn Sheep! Eight of them! No one I know has ever actually seen big horn sheep and here were eight of them! As I passed, they lifted their heads in greeting... a Sign perhaps? But what do they mean? No, just happenstance.

I rounded a curve and there is another very large Ram. This time he is looking straight at me, watching as I pass.

OK, what is it?

"We are strong. We endure the winters and understand the heights. We deal with thin air, and still are sure footed in high places that man is afraid to even try to reach. We know the quiet heights of the eagle with our feet on the ground.

"You find our mating rituals amusing as we butt our heads for the right mate. Is man so different in that respect? We, at least, seldom harm each other in the process. Men and women seem to enjoy the process of 'butting' heads and ignore any harm it may cause.

"There is much we could share with you.

"There is the peace and confidence of moving through and experiencing the heights while touching a tangible reality. This is a skill man could benefit from.

"Can I possibly give you the feeling of having more sky around you than earth, while earth is solid beneath your feet. Sounds you create reaching out into the sky and returning as clearly as they were sent out, doubled, tripled, many voiced, demonstrating the laws of the universe, crisp, clean and clearly present?

"When clouds cover our mountains, we see them coming and know what they are, knowing always what is beyond. And even when our vision is limited, still we find our footing in the rocks.

"We have a way of knowing balance in all situations, even in munching grass by the side of a highway."

Perhaps there is a way of being able to handle the heights of being without losing touch with the earth. Maybe it is possible to deal with all the struggles connected with living, without losing my spiritual footing and crashing into the deep chasms I have associated with that process.

COYOTE

In my travels I use my solitary driving time for self excavation—personal archaeology, unearthing relics of being I recognize as still operational even though they were long ago outmoded. During this process I feel "pulled" to the side of the road, where I find the carcass of a dead coyote. As I impulsively reach out and touch its fur it seems to lift its head and begin speaking. It speaks of the patterns of being I had been examining, and how much of my life had involved self trickery, outsmarting myself and hiding truth from myself, seeking illusions when the truth was within my grasp. He told me how the coyote in me was now dead and my truths were emerging. At first I feel encouraged and feel I am really making some progress... then I pull back and think, "Perhaps so, but this coyote is dead too, and still lifted its head to speak!"

The coyote laughed and said, *"Exactly!"*

"Man will forever be capable of twisting his own truths. Never lose sight of the possibility of being totally wrong.

"Only by questioning everything you think and feel do you even have a chance at maintaining balance and objectivity, and even then you can subtly distort what is real. That subtle distortion can make even the richest insight a total fallacy."

I thought about what he was saying, and said, "All right, without questioning we have little hope of seeing truth. But, to analyze and try to figure things out can create larger fallacies—the very process of questioning and probing can hurl you further into the world of distortion. So, What is the answer?" I asked. "To accept without question leads to distortion and to question and examine leads to distortion. Where is the path to truth?"

Again the Coyote laughed, *"Exactly!"*

"Your foolishness will always be your downfall.

"Balance is the key. The quiet peacefulness of balance and neutrality where you do not 'need' it to be anything; where you do not question too harshly and simply accept your own clear answers. Somewhere between is the quiet place where truth will shine with clarity, and you will know.

"You have the answers within you... you merely need to find that place where things quietly fall into place...

"And, to ask the right questions!"

Ah, but that is the hard part!

DOG

I found myself feeling anger about an object that had been deliberately destroyed. It had been old, full of old medicine and I had felt it was one of my ceremonial pieces. I felt my medicine had been attacked and somehow diminished by the act. More than that, the lack of respect in this act of destruction, and others, felt like a diminishment of me. Even though I felt the wrongness of the actions were worthy of concern, I was still attempting to look outward to deal with it. I was missing something.

There was something within I was not addressing... something I was not seeing....

And then Dog began speaking in my ear.

"Do not put your medicine into things. They can be taken or destroyed. Do not draw power from things. Power must be within if it is to be valid and clear.

"Does the wolf require an eagle feather to be in his power? Does an eagle need a pipe for his medicine?

"We carry it all within, only there can it be pure, unviolated and strong beyond measure. Animal medicine can show you how. Animals know this clarity. We also

know the corruption possible, for the dog was once wolf and coyote. In succumbing to the corruption and weakness of need and security we have become something different. Still we are animal and cling to our own being. The dog is one who chose to help man while keeping in touch with his own animal, and he gave up freedom and wildness to do this.

"In the process we lost much, but we have also gained for we have kept our intent clean. We chose to be with humans and if we have the opportunity to be ourselves at all, we will stay with our humans through all adversity and continue to teach as our underlying wolfness dictates.

"You can use things in your medicine to assist you (things being items or people), adding their medicine to yours. But if you rely on them to complete your magic or to make it whole, you have weakened your being. If the power is not within you, then you have no power.

"Remember the internal solitude of being, and the basic animal nature of it. Even social animals are still beings of internal solitude. No illusion of closeness changes that, not even the reality of closeness changes that. We must all face ourselves in solitude, choose our paths in solitude, and find our own truths in solitude. Only in that truth of being can we offer truth. Still, no matter how true it may be, if we have need, or fear, or feel insecure, or have any other ego pressures, it becomes distorted and destructive. It cannot matter whether the offered truth is seen or accepted or it is not offered from a place of clarity—even though the principle of seeing and accepting truth matters a great deal.

"In Nature, animals face life and death in solitude. Assistance is always welcome, but it is not relied on for being. We make do with what we have and are, and ask nothing. Our spirit selves reach into the void for any additional help we get, and we accept what is given. The pain of lack is lived with—or not. No matter. It is the process of life that matters, not the outcome, even when *the outcome is life or death, success or failure, approval or rejection, love or hostility, health or mutilation, abundance or starvation, comfort or torture. However, the outcome is also predicated on the clarity of the process.*

"No one knows the process within you but you. Only you can determine what is true in your solitude, and if you are wrong you will pay for it. Even though your untruths will affect all those you touch, it will be their solitude that will decide what to do with them. Your truth, or lack of it, is for you alone.

"However your patterns will be obvious to those around you and their choices will be made from what you demonstrate.

"Ultimately, it will be the magic of your own truth, or lack of it, that will save you or damn you, no matter what is inflicted on you by others.

"And, when you truly understand this you will not attempt to inflict your truth or how you think things should be on others.

"You may offer it, but you will KNOW that their solitude will decide what to do with it. Your power is not to CHANGE anything. Your power will only add or take away, offering ways of opening or closing doors.

"Your power does not even CHANGE you. It is always the quiet choices that make changes within, allowing the power to be and using it accordingly.

"Does your power add to life or does it create destruction? If it destroys, does it eliminate barriers to life or does it attack life itself? These are questions to ask in solitude about your own being and what is happening in the world you inhabit."

Yes, wrongful acts by others are worthy of our concern, and may place obstacles in our path. But if the power is within they cannot touch it. It is only my own anger and fear that diminishes me! If I am clear, and work in harmony with the universe I am as strong as I ever was. And, in overcoming the obstacles without fear or anger, I grow stronger.

RACCOON

I was sitting in my living room when I heard the thumps and bumps. It was the family of raccoons assaulting the cat food outside my glass doors. They know me, so that when I turned on the light and opened the curtain they reacted with no more than normal awareness. This time one of them came over to the door and began pawing at it, sat down and looked at me intensely, so I asked what it wanted to tell me.

"We are adaptable. We survive even in cities while remaining wild and maintaining our identity. Fear has little to do with our survival, we rely on our internal balance to cope with each situation. We are not threatened by wilderness or civilization. We can move in either one freely.

"We are conscious of family and its importance, but we are also able to move comfortably on our own. We eat what is available, cleansing it our own way.

"Take care. Be alert to change around you. Do not try to function as though in a forest when surrounded by pavement. And as you move through different worlds, mask your eyes, but see clearly. What is happening in the life force and flow around you? How

100

is it influencing you and your actions? How much effort must be applied to maintain the directions appropriate to you? Is your own path clear? Can you find your way through the currents and distractions? Learning to shift from one lifestyle to another and back again can be useful if you understand what you are doing and why.

"But if you tend to become lost in the internal process of shifting ground you must learn to find your own anchor points to help you know who you are and where you need to be going as you pass through the different currents of energy pushing you this way and that.

"Where do you go? Where do you come from? Where are you now? Life is both simple and extremely complex, but once the tricks of balance are known, the simplicity is clear. Until then the confusion can disintegrate one's being.

"What is it you want? The lesson will always be balance.

"We can always find our balance even when pursued by a predator—can you?"

You are pursued by predators... just as we are pursued by life's problems and complexities that prey on our sense of self.

Yes, I am constantly learning lessons of balance. I become more and more aware of forces that attack that balance, any of which can cause me to fall.

LIZARD

A customer decided she would rather come to me and see what I am offering rather than have me carry my cases around to her at the mall.

As I sat outside waiting for her, enjoying the early spring weather, a lizard ran across my foot. It stopped on the top of my shoe, looked at me and pulled at my attention.

I found myself looking through its eyes— close to the ground and somewhat slanted. Then I could feel my vision change, looking down from a height, and lizard began to explain.

"We have the ability to see things from different vantage points: either low to the ground or from a great height. We are light enough and agile enough to reach even the topmost branches of a tree. We can climb under eaves of houses or beneath branches and see things upside down if we want to. Whatever we want to look at, we can see from any angle we choose.

"Birds can shift their vantage point, but they must lose touch with the earth to really see things differently. They are also constantly moving and only briefly watch something from any particular perspective and must assimilate what they see very quickly.

"We never lose our connection with the earth and

can examine things as long as we need to. We can shift our point of observation however we feel necessary in order to ponder and analyze what we see.

"Both methods are of value, but people tend to want to soar, losing touch with the earth and seeing only briefly. Then they become frustrated by having only moments of sight. When they try to stabilize the vision the movement stops and they fall".

"In lizard sight you can hold the vantage point as long as you want, while continuing to feel the flow of life through your feet. You are always in contact with the earth even while exploring lofty visions.

"Our feet are an integral part of the experience. We have senses in our feet as well as the ability to grip and climb where we choose. In whatever our feet touch we can sense the flow of life itself and are aware of subtle shifts in that flow as well as subtle changes in vibration. Part of our vision is in our eyes, and part is in our feet, which makes our awareness constantly keen."

You are right. No single sense or perspective can see us through the complex patterns we deal with everyday. We must integrate a variety of information in making our choices and decisions, being ready to shift and change instaneously when new information makes it advisable.

Stay with me Lizard... help me remember the full spectrum of senses and perspectives that I have access to.

DRAGONFLY

I had been working seven days a week from the time I got up until I went to bed for a long time. I needed a break in the intensity and constant effort.

So, my son and I took our rafts and floated down a section of the river we live near.

It was a relaxed lazy day that my spirit drank in hungrily.

Dragonflies flew on the surface of the river and they landed on my bare knees.

A very large one settled on my arm, and as I was noticing that I did not feel the touch of even this large one, it spoke:

"Yes, we touch life very lightly.

"When we fly we work very hard with our wings, but we still touch life lightly in order to sense the slightest shifts in energy so we can tell how to apply our efforts."

OK, thank you!

I have been grabbing the reins and pushing again.

Relax, move lightly, and be aware of rocks and trees, flowing with the river, following the currents so I can stay in the main channel, the deep channel, and move most effectively.

PAY BACK

Animals have become a part of my daily life. In my gratitude for their teachings I asked them how I could balance their gifts.

I had already been working with animal spirits along the road and experienced their calls for help.

Their calls always resulted in elaborate experiences, including carrying a hawk that had lost its flight feathers on my lap for a full day while hunting a place where it could be cared for until its feathers grew back.

But I wanted to do more.

Their response was a surprise!

I had been a vegetarian for some time, simply because my body no longer seemed to tolerate meat. The animals asked me to eat meat again!

As they explained it to me, they have no problem with being killed and eaten. That is part of a natural process that they understand and accept. But the way it is now done has no awareness, no honor, no respect for their being. They are callously and even cruelly slaughtered, with no thought given to them as living beings, much less any attention given to their spirits. And, then they are cut into pieces that conveniently allow people to ignore that these pieces were once an animal.

They asked that I eat the meat and supply the honor and respect the animals had been denied.

I replied that I became ill when eating meat, I did not think I could physically do it.

105

They said they would take care of that, that the process would shift the energies so my body would no longer be offended.

I have eaten meat since then with no further problems. Except when I forget for any reason to "talk" to the animal.

This talking to the animals I eat has resulted in some strange occurrences.

Once in a restaurant I was having a solitary thanksgiving meal. I received my plate and began laughing out loud.

As I had reached for the turkey I encountered:

"Duh... what happened? I was just looking around at the sky and WHUMP! I'm here!"

I said, "You're dead."

"Ohhh," he said. *"Bummer!"*

On the whole my involvement with animals has become an accepted occurrence. They step in and speak or show themselves as I am pondering a problem or brush me with their spirit just to say "HI." When I see an animal my first thought is to touch their mind to see what is going on. Or, as I am going through life and encountering various situations their images will flash in my mind, reminding me of some teaching or other. They are something I now simply take for granted as a part of my life.

RAVEN
AND CROW

I had been extremely busy. I had not made any deliberate contact with an animal in quite some time. As I sat down to do some paper work the image of crow placed itself in my mind. Then it seemed to be raven and then back to crow, and the words formed in my mind.

"We have noticed that you have a difficult time being able to tell the difference between us when we fly around you."

I laughed, agreeing with them and waited for more. When nothing came, I assumed it was just one of those brief contacts and went back to work.

Again the image of crow superimposed with raven occurred. I was puzzled. I thought they had said all they had to say. I said, "Yes, I heard you." The image persisted and with a feeling of irritation

They said, *"Start writing this down!"*

"Oh, sorry." And I reached for pen and paper as the words began to flow.

"It is not surprising that you have difficulty in telling us apart. We are very similar, and we deal with much the same things. Our wisdom has to do with the laws of spirit and nature. The only difference is that one leans toward the structure of the law and the other deals more with the 'magic' of it. These are simply two aspects of the same thing.

"As in your world, if you understand the structure of the law you have the choice of following it to the letter, or

bending it to your own purposes. And if you bend it, you can do it with the intent of feeding life or denying life.

"In our world, all laws have divine purpose, and the bending of those laws to support life's current needs is all within the structure of law. We do not break the laws— we cannot. We are not even able go against them without severe repercussions. The laws snap back into place and we would be caught in the middle after creating unpleasant vortexes in the energies.

"Man-made laws have little to do with these divine energies and are created out of a clumsy attempt to define and enforce divine law which needs no enforcing and protects itself.

"Yet even with man's laws, when they are broken, there are consequences. The difference is that with man's laws it is possible to avoid repercussions if you can avoid being caught breaking them. With divine law, there is no avoiding being caught!

"Magic is lawful in the divine sense. It is the process of taking the flows of energy and directing them toward a purpose, but not changing the flows, or the intent of the law.

" If you attempt to go against the natural currents, or redirect energy flows for personal purposes that arise from an ego source with no real connection to the divine intent, you place yourself at risk. And any such interference with a divine flow of life is covered by divine law and will automatically result in the proper responses.

"Surrender to Divine law gives you connection and a sense of what can and cannot be done within its structure. Without this surrender and the understanding that you CONTROL nothing, you are playing a game that will result in one kind of pain or another.

"Recognize and accept the natural order of things and whatever you do will be in harmony with it."

Yes, I had once again been trying to push the river and direct it where I wanted it to go. I must relax and trust.

WOLVERINE

A friend asked me to talk to wolverine and see what they have to say. I felt no personal connection and so it hung there as a question for a while. Then as I was driving south of Dallas, wolverine arrogantly nudged me with his nose indicating he was ready to talk now. I was filled with a feeling of irritation and vague insult as he demanded that I stop immediately. He inspired instant hostility and I wondered how much of this feeling was mine and how much was his.

"We tend to avoid man— they are too much like us in nature.

"We are both predators that are slow and clumsy. Both man and wolverine must rely on craft and cunning to survive. We must think things through and plan our strategy when we hunt because we have no speed or agility to take our prey. But the wolverine practices hunting every day so we are masters of the hunt and masters at thinking things through, and are experts in the field of strategy. Man thinks he is unique in this but he seldom develops it to an art as we do.

"Because we understand this side of man we do not fear him, we are better at it than he is. Consequently, we do not hesitate to prey on humans, if we choose to. We are the only natural predators of man and if we decide to hunt one down he must draw on every resource he has in order to have even a chance at survival.

"Once we decide on a goal, we will

pursue it relentlessly until we achieve it. We pursue with infinite patience knowing that with our craft and cunning we will eventually succeed in our quest, even if it takes many plots and plans and circuitous routes to get us there. The only way we will not achieve our goal is if we change our mind and decide to redirect our energies. But we do not make any decisions lightly and seldom change our mind.

"We have even more tenacity than that of our cousins the badgers, but we are not as peaceful as they are and we do not have their gentle natures. Like man, we will fight for the sake of fighting.

"Be grateful that we have few young. There is nothing that can stand in our way successfully. Man's supremacy would be threatened if we existed in greater numbers.

"Also, be grateful that we are solitary and tend to see man as a prey we are bored with because they are no real challenge. Even animals in the wild with predictable instincts are more of a challenge than human beings. Show us that you have the wit to be an adversary worth our attention and we may accept the challenge. Otherwise you are simply not worth the bother."

As I felt him arrogantly stalk off with all his confidence and self assurance I could feel my smoldering anger. Then I realized, in his overbearing manner, he did not exhibit the free flowing respect I had felt with other animals. He did not give respect and he neither asked for nor expected it from humans. He would not have valued it if he got it unless you proved to him you had enough discernment to know what you were giving. You would have to prove a great deal to him in order to earn any kind of respect from him.

As I said, my first reaction was a kind of outrage. But then, what makes us so special? It is only our own arrogance that makes us think we are. And our arrogance is based more on illusion and what we tell ourselves than it is on action and results. The "king" of a city has learned to make his way among his own kind... place him anywhere out of this setting and he would not know how to survive. He would discover that he does not have the creative thinking process he thought he did.

Yet, other animals have been able to thrive in our cities. Surely a wolverine placed in the environment of a city would be able to figure out precisely what he needed to do in a brief period of time and become a serious problem for the people who lived in its territory.

My anger cooled to acceptance and understanding, and once again my willingness to learn from and appreciate the wolverine as another aspect of life's flow returned. I began to see the importance of what he had to say.

Make decisions only after giving time and thought to them. If something is worth your attention and your pursuit then do not give up. Use every resource of your mind to pursue that goal and do not be impatient for results. There are times when self-assurance and confidence can carry you through setbacks that would shatter many people. I need to cultivate these things within myself.

Do I find the wolverine threatening? Perhaps I find Man threatening as well!

Am I not as innately capable as any of them? Am I perhaps too peaceful at times, too willing to yield and dispense respect? Perhaps I should be a bit more reserved and demand that respect be earned. Perhaps I need to be firmly aggressive, even hostile at times.

Somewhere in the middle is the balance point, I think. I have let myself be intimidated, at times, purely because of my own lack of confidence. And while my principles dictate that respect is the right of all life, there are deeper levels of respect that must be earned.

And, my heart must remember that even crippled animals have the tools to survive. I have all that I need to face even a wolverine, but having tools means nothing if I do not use them!

111

Abilities may vary in each individual, but each has enough! Only our own timidity prevents us from using what we have!

And, bottom line—if I were going to be honest, I had to admit that his arrogance offended me because I had begun to feel arrogant about MY animals and how they were so willing to be of help to ME. So special... I had come to expect the soft and gentle respect and help they offered me. What had I done to earn it? What had I done to deserve all their concern and support? Isn't my arrogant assumption that I am given their wisdom because I am so special, one of the things they have warned me about? Have they not told me that their gifts are merely part of the flow of life and they are given in the spirit of cooperation that is offered to anyone willing to receive them?

Thank you wolverine, you have reminded me of another one of my self defeating aspects.

EARTHWORM

While doing business with a customer who became an instant friend, we continued talking after our business was concluded. When I found my car blocked so I had to wait even longer before I could leave, I felt no irritation because it meant we were able to continue our conversation. As the course of discussions turned to animals and their teachings, she told me one of her totem animals was the earthworm. I found this fascinating and said I had never heard of an earthworm totem before. I asked her what it meant. She said no one else had ever heard of it either and she had had to sort it out for herself.

She said the earthworm told her they moved through the earth, taking it in, processing it, and removing impurities. Then they return it clean, enriched, and purified.

What a wonderful totem to have!

That night I dreamed of the worm. The image and feeling was how the worm was intimately involved with the earth. Essentially its whole existence revolved around making love to her and helping her living entity in the process of the gargantuan task of being the source of all physical life.

Can you imagine being so completely devoted to service? Earthworms are totally harmless. They live in humility and yet have a strong sense of self with no arrogance or pride. These are beings of a holy order that make all our self-sacrificing human endeavors toward service seem pale.

Is there any other being that is as thoughtful and supportive of the earth, mother of us all?

LIZARD AGAIN

A friend was asking me about change and talking about how difficult it was to let go of old habits and patterns.

As I listened, a lizard caught my eye. It laughed, waved its tail and skittered up the wall. In its laugh, it had communicated a much more detailed message, and the translation of it began to form its words in my mouth.

The lizard has a long tail. They like their tails. They are rather attached to them.

When a predator is pursuing them, if they are caught it is usually by their tail. At a time like this, the lizard has the choice: do I let myself be eaten because I have such an attachment to my tail, or do I give it up? The lizard will choose to break off his tail, escape the predator and grow a new one.

We are faced with the same dilemma many times in our lives. Do we let an attachment cause us to be devoured, or do we let go and grow a new one? We have a choice, just as lizards do. Isn't it better to give up something that has been important to us when it becomes a threat to our welfare rather than be consumed by holding on?

Look to the lizards. Perhaps they can help us with the process of breaking things off when we need to.

THE GATHERING

Nothing was working right. Obstacles were everywhere. It seemed I could not take successful action in any direction. One thing after another went wrong.

My car was just one example. In a three month period it developed a sound in the engine no one seemed able to diagnose.

One afternoon, at almost five o'clock, antifreeze began spurting through a pinhole in a hose, which blossomed into a race to get the proper part and find someone who could fix it before the antifreeze was depleted and the car overheated. The next day I had all the hoses replaced.

Tires began disintegrating beneath me, with tread flying across the highway.

There was a definite power loss so I took it into the local dealership to see if they could do anything. They kept it five hours. As I waited for the outcome I watched the mechanics wander around the garage and wondered if anyone was going to do any real work on my car. They charged me $350 (including five hours of labor cost). There was some improvement in the car but the problem remained. I took it back and told them it was not fixed. They looked at it, checked it and said there was nothing wrong with it. I then went to another mechanic and when he opened the hood, he pointed to the spark plugs showing me two wires that were completely disconnected! He connected the wires, tuned the engine and the car was again working properly.

Shortly after that, I stopped at the post office. When I came out, the car would not start. Of course it was nearly five o'clock again!

Once the starter was replaced, I felt the streak of luck was over and went out on a business trip. The antilock brake system went out, the air conditioner ran hot, another tire went bad, and the speedometer and gauges began acting weird.

Back home, with the most recent batch of problems resolved, the car began starting sluggishly, which required a new battery.

Meanwhile, the sound in the engine continued. I decided that whatever it was may be part of all the other problems and decided to have the garage take a serious look at it. I was told I needed a new engine.

The cost of a new engine was about the same amount I owed on the car. So I began to shop for a new one. In the middle of this process, I stopped for groceries and came out to find another hose had exploded and all my antifreeze was on the ground in a puddle beneath my car.

Every aspect of my life was functioning like this.

I felt frustrated, bogged down with too much mundane garbage and I was sinking fast. I felt isolated and overworked. My abilities to lift myself out of this sinkhole were wearing thin and I began spiraling downward, feeling very justified in my self-pity. I knew my attitude was not helping matters, but the constant stress was getting to me.

At first, in my depression, I did not notice the animals that began appearing.

My house seemed full of spiders and spider webs. Rabbits were sitting in my driveway every time I drove up to my house. Mockingbirds kept flashing at me. Squirrels were suddenly jumping all over my porch. Buzzards circled my house. Turtles were all over the back roads.

When I found a bright green grasshopper sitting on top of my shampoo bottle in my shower I began to think something might be going on and started to listen to more than my self-pity.

I noticed flies were landing on me again and whispering, *"You are forgetting to clean your energy."*

As I drove my rural road absorbed in my internal world I did not notice a small snake and ran over it. I felt terrible about it, so I stopped to apologize. I found that it was a miniature version of the rattlesnake I had talked to and he spoke in my ear, *"Be careful of what you say AND think. Your own poison can kill you."*

A lizard appeared on my kitchen window as I was washing dishes. It said, *"Shift your perspective and let go!"*

Raccoons attacked the cat food by my glass doors saying, *"Find your balance!"*

Dragonflies landed on me as I went to and from the car saying, *"Lighten up!"*

Robins hopped around me telling me not to lose touch with my natural self.

As I began following their recommendations, relaxing into a more neutral state, the gathering of animal spirits and their advice continued.

Bear said, *"You are trying to change winter."*

Coyote said, *"Your self-deception is distorting how you see what is going on. You can defeat yourself very easily this way."*

Raven and crow spoke together, *"No one can break true laws, no matter what it seems like."*

Badger said, *"Hang on and open new ways."*

Wolf said, *"Look to your pack, and accept help from them."*

Dog reminded me, *"Your power is within. Do not allow outside influences to determine your thoughts and actions. Remember your solitude and find your power there."*

Big Horn sheep said, *"Stay grounded, but remember the heights."*

Wolverine stormed through saying, *"Don't be so timid and weak! Use the tools you have! You can find a strategy to attack any problem, if you do not quit!"*

Earthworm quietly moved in and said, *"Serve Life!"*

I felt a stirring of courage within myself.

How could I continue to allow myself to wallow in self-pity and depression with all this support?

Just go to the next thing on the list and continue trying. The results are not my responsibility. The process and what I put into it are the only parts over which I have any control. Do what I feel is necessary and maintain effort.

So I continued to strive and cope with setbacks, waiting for "winter" to pass.

BUFFALO

The book was basically finished and Steve began working on the illustrations for it. During a creative burst, a composite drawing appeared and we both agreed it was perfect for the cover—except that one of the main animals featured was a buffalo, and I had not written anything for buffalo.

We both liked the drawing as it was. Steve's answer was simple. "Well, write something."

I had not felt buffalo volunteering and tried to say the buffalo on the cover could stand for the animals people could talk to on their own, but the "pressure" to write something for buffalo continued.

I began thinking about the buffalo and all that seems to be connected with it: how it was the local supermarket for so many Native Americans. This was where they found much of the material of their daily lives: not only food, but clothing, housing, and tools. Every part of the buffalo was used. And in their gratitude for the gifts there was honor and respect given to the animal and its spirit.

When the white man came along they saw the buffalo only as potential profit and systematically slaughtered them.

Even here the fate of the buffalo and the Native Americans had parallel paths.

I thought of White Buffalo Calf Woman bringing gifts and how the white buffalo is considered sacred—and then I remembered that I had spoken with one buffalo.

When, after many years, a white buffalo was born and survived, I made a pilgrimage to see it. By the time I was able to get there over a year had gone by and the baby white buffalo was now brown. She was distinguishable only if you knew what to look for.

As I watched her peers push her into a corner I reached out to her with my mind. I could feel the others being irritated with her and how she was peacefully tolerating it.

I expressed surprise at her treatment by the others, while the questions about her coloring hovered in my mind. She looked at me and I had a flash of understanding that her treatment by the herd was their way of handling all the adulation that had been aimed at her. It was their way of reminding her she was part of the herd, and she must not let these ideas cause her to think she was "special."

I said, "But you ARE special!"

She responded with, *"Yes, but if I think so, I won't be. What they do is a gift to help me remain the White Buffalo in my heart."*

"But why are you not white outside?" I asked.

"Those who wish to see me for what I am will recognize me. Those who wish to harm me for what I am will not. They will think I no longer matter because I no longer fit their image of what they think I should be.

"It is protection, while protection is needed. When it is time, I will again be everything they think I should be. For now, my herd helps me hold onto what I am where it matters."

I said, "In other words, keep a low profile until you can make a difference."

"I am only a symbol. I will not do anything, but I will have meaning for those who will make changes happen."

Of course, this is what symbols are for: to stimulate actions in those for whom they have meaning.

Animals who have shared knowledge have meaning for me. The power is not in the animal itself, but in what they mean to me and the consequent action that meaning stimulates. They have become models and images for ideas and reminders of the action I want to take in my life.

121

WHERE DO WE GO FROM HERE?

With all the experiences recounted in this book, I still wondered how much was "real." Was this just my inner being trying to speak to me and finding this avenue one that was effective?

Perhaps.

I could explain away most of it on that basis. Even picking up a wild hawk and carrying it around on my lap.

Then one day I was cleaning the yard. I picked up an old wagon one of the kids had left there for about a year. A large coachwhip snake about eight or ten feet long was under it. We startled the heck out of each other and we both took off in opposite directions.

I stopped, turned around and went back. I reached out to him with my mind and voice, telling the snake I was sorry. I did not mean to disturb him or frighten him and he was welcome there so please come back.

And he did. He moved to within two feet of me and coiled up very peacefully.

We both remained there having a conversation.

He showed me how he uses his tail in the weeds to sound like a rattler.

I laughed and told him it was a good trick, but I knew he was not a rattler and he had no poison.

During the conversation my dog came slowly around me and moved closer to the snake.

I turned and told her to be nice, the snake was welcome here.

She gave me a dirty look that said, "I know that!"

She then also moved to within two feet of the snake and lay down very respectfully. The three of us establishing a close triangle.

After a while I went back to cleaning the yard and the dog and snake stayed there together, watching me all afternoon.

By evening I went back and thanked the snake. This experience had given me validation that the communication was real on some level. I could find no other explanation for this occurrence.

Since then, I have not seriously questioned the communications, and operated as if it were fact.

I am by no means unique in regard to having such communications. Many times I hit stretches of road where I have no work to do with animals who are the victims of cars lying along the sides. Others have been there before me and there are no spirits to work with because they have already been helped on their way.

When I mention talking to animals, many people will respond by telling me their experiences and the lessons they have learned, which are always different from mine.

Our mutual interpretations of each animal usually make sense, even though symbology and meaning may differ from person to person

You can make your own connections. Just open your heart, listen to it, and follow its lead.

INDEX OF
ANIMAL LESSONS

MOCKINGBIRD	Choose your own song
MOUSE	Risk
OWL	Shadow self
RABBIT	Fear
RACCOON	Balance
RATTLESNAKE	Poison
RAVEN	Magic
REDBIRDS	Abundance
ROBIN	Natural connection
SNAKE	Shedding skins
SPIDER	Life web
SQUIRREL	Gravity
TURKEY	Giveaway
TURTLE	Defensiveness
WOLF	Relationships
WOLVERINE	Strategy

ABOUT THE AUTHOR

Susan Wells was born in Grand Rapids, Minnesota. The town of Grand Rapids had one claim to fame: Judy Garland was born there. When Susan learned this about her birth place she felt that surely by being born in such an obscure place with this kind of "history" something was added to the simple fact of birth. So Susan lived her life with the taste of fame and fortune at the back of her throat.

But, as time passed and she tried being many different people: housewife, office worker, mother, artisan, actress, dancer, telephone operator, nurse, baker, minister, business woman, etc., the taste at the back of her throat began to grow stale. And, after 50 years of trying to be somebody, she decided that all the credentials and letters after her name weren't really her after all and perhaps just being was good enough. Writing has been one of the few consistent elements over the years, with sporadic attempts at publication. Some attempts were successful, but life kept getting in the way of being serious about writing, so it took eight years to produce her first real book: *Earthborn Wisdom.*

ABOUT THE ARTIST

Steve was raised in rural Kansas and Northeastern Oklahoma. Studying avenues of thought and possibilities from early youth built respect for efforts of sincerity in unveiling the unknown. From beginnings in Christianity to experiencing realities within Cherokee life, the blood within and the occurrence of experience validated realms called impossible. While experiencing an extreme childhood, animals were one physical being that always offered assistance in times of despair. Innocent, true and non-judgemental, they assisted and allowed me to openly express my true being. When respect is given to another, floods of information are at our disposal.

In 1988 I was fortunate and came into contact with nature in the form of lightning. It was a wonderful opportunity to truly face myself, challenge my foundation of thought and validate what had previously been only a possibility. While participating in traditional healing ceremonies, giving talks on the use of words, truth, honesty and purpose, I have provided symbolic expressions in the United States and internationally. From drums, vases, eggs, spheres, jewelry, and quartz etchings the symbolism has been a source of learning and enjoyment. The value we find with symbolism establishes value within ourselves.

ALSO AVAILABLE

PRINTS

full page illustrations available as prints

NOTECARDS

STATIONARY

For more information contact

DREAMTIME PUBLISHING

P.O. Box 834
Tahlequah, Ok. 74465